It takes a brave man to take on the sin of envy I
is largely built on the exploitation and expansi(
Fabarez is that brave man. In this faithful book, filled with biblical and pastoral wisdom, Fabarez gets right to the heart of the issue and offers keen anal-
ysis and trustworthy teaching. I highly commend this book to all believers.

**R. ALBERT MOHLER JR.**
President, Southern Baptist Theological Seminary

This book is simply excellent. Mike Fabarez has tackled a neglected topic
and successfully made the case that we all have a bigger problem with envy
than we would like to admit. Using scriptural examples and imperatives, he
reminds us of the biblical bottom line that "love does not envy." What a difference it would make if we eradicated the envy lurking in our sinful hearts
and truly cultivated love of neighbor. Pastor Mike's well organized work
written with a pastoral heart not only illuminates the problem but carefully
provides a plan of counterattack. His insights into how we unknowingly
provoke others to envy are striking too. He's right. I did not know I had a
problem with envy. I do. I am glad to have this wise counsel to both admon-
ish and encourage me.

**MARY K. MOHLER**
Wife of Albert Mohler; author of *Growing in Gratitude* and *Susannah
Spurgeon*

With precise biblical insight, this book, which is skillfully written and mas-
terfully illustrated, aids the reader in dealing with a universal core problem. It aims to not only inform but also to transform us to comprehend
and experience the love of God in a fresh way—the love that uniquely
frees us to know ourselves, be ourselves, and enjoy ourselves to the glory
of the God who alone never disappoints!

**BILL THRASHER**
Author and professor, Moody Theological Seminary

It's easy today to find resources focusing on sinful practices that impact
our lives like an exploding bomb, damaging all within reach. What's not
so common is a book like this that tackles a sin that affects every one of us
and is far more subtle in its destructive power. With the Bible as his source

and guide, Mike Fabarez exposes the sin of envy and then offers a powerful remedy for its seductive influence in our lives.

**ED STETZER**
Dean, Talbot School of Theology

Few people understand the devastating power of envy. As a homicide detective, I repeatedly encountered it as a common motivation for the murders I investigated. But that's not where the real danger lies. It's in the everyday, insidious way envy creeps into the lives of those of us who will never commit a homicide. In *Envy*, Dr. Mike Fabarez illustrates the cost envy extracts from all of us and outlines a biblical strategy to overcome its corrosive influence. If you've ever struggled with envy, jealousy, or covetousness, *Envy* will help you chart a path to freedom.

**J. WARNER WALLACE**
*Dateline* featured cold-case detective, author, speaker, senior fellow at the Colson Center for Christian Worldview, and Adjunct Professor of Apologetics at Talbot School of Theology (Biola University), Gateway Seminary, and Southern Evangelical Seminary

Envy is one of those "respectable sins." It's easy to underassess its sinfulness and to underestimate the spiritual damage it does in our lives. That's why I'm thankful Mike Fabarez has written *Envy*. This book will help the reader detect envy within them, deal with it, and pursue a more faithful, satisfied life in Christ. These reasons and more are why I heartily recommend this book.

**JASON K. ALLEN**
President, Midwestern Baptist Theological Seminary & Spurgeon College

If I weren't thoroughly warned, I would be tempted to envy this excellent book by Mike Fabarez. It's everything you want in a spiritual study: engaging, lively, hilarious in places, wise, humble, and above all drenched in biblical truth. Throughout, I marveled at Fabarez's communicative gifts; he has a serious God-given ability to relate to the reader, simplify the complex, and exhort the sleeping. Best of all, his call to kill envy is steeped in the powerful grace of God, which changes envious and self-worshiping creatures like us into glad-hearted servants of our Lord and Savior Jesus Christ.

**OWEN STRACHAN**
Coauthor, *The Essential Jonathan Edwards*; provost, Grace Bible Theological Seminary

I just finished reading my friend Pastor Mike Fabarez's new book, *Envy*, and boy, do I wish I had written it. And therein lies the problem. We need this book because we all struggle with envy at times—wishing we had stuff others have or accomplished work others have achieved or obtained status others have earned. God wants us to learn contentment and reject envy in our own lives. Read Pastor Mike's biblical and practical study of envy. If we apply the concepts contained in it, we'll not only learn and grow in contentment, but we'll deepen our walk with the Lord Jesus.

**MICHAEL RYDELNIK**
VP and Academic Dean, Professor of Jewish Studies and Bible, Moody Bible Institute; host and Bible teacher, Moody Radio's *Open Line with Dr. Michael Rydelnik*

Most people have more stuff than ever yet feel less content. Why? Mike Fabarez challenges us to examine our hearts to look for envy, which may be robbing us of our contentment and our joy. As a friend, Mike has always inspired me to love God more and grow in spiritual maturity. As an author, he will challenge us all to evaluate our desires and replace envy with love and rejoicing. If you love Jesus and want to be more like Him, I encourage you to read this book!

**THOMAS WHITE**
President and Professor of Theology, Cedarville University

Someone once wisely said that envy is the last sin to die. Dr. Mike Fabarez gives weight to this truth by citing many instances in Scripture that point to this deadly sin. I especially appreciated chapter 7 and the epilogue. As a teacher and counselor of women, I look forward to having this resource.

**SUSAN HECK**
Author, counselor, teacher (www.withthemaster.org)

Like a spiritual cancer silently eroding the strength of our souls, I am convinced envy is a great enemy of many Christians who don't even know they have the disease. In this book, Mike Fabarez functions as a true physician of the soul, diagnosing the terrible sin of envy that exists in each of our hearts and prescribing the strong cure that exists in Christ alone. I hope you will read it and share it with others.

**HEATH LAMBERT**
Senior Pastor at First Baptist Church, Jacksonville, FL

The title says it all: *Envy: A Big Problem You Didn't Know You Had*. In this book, Mike Fabarez uncovers layers of rationalization and shows that yes, we all struggle with the hidden sin of envy. He exposes this sin but also shows us the way to freedom so that we can rejoice when we hear good news about others who are more successful than we! This is a very thoughtful book; read it, and let it touch your life.

**ERWIN W. LUTZER**
Pastor Emeritus, The Moody Church, Chicago

In *Envy*, Mike Fabarez addresses a common but often overlooked sin in a solidly biblical way and with a pastor's heart. This book will help anyone wanting to kill this pernicious sin that kills gratitude, joy, and fruitfulness.

**ERIK THOENNES**
Professor of Theology, Talbot School of Theology / Biola University; pastor, Grace Evangelical Free Church, La Mirada, CA; author of *Godly Jealousy: A Theology of Intolerant Love* and *Life's Biggest Questions: What the Bible Says About the Things That Matter Most*

Pastor Mike Fabarez is an extraordinary Bible teacher and perceptive analyzer of today's culture. With candor and spiritual insight, Pastor Mike exposes a deadly camouflaged enemy wreaking havoc on many personal lives, relationships, and communities. I highly recommend this book because it will not only help you identify the symptoms of envy possibly embedded in your own heart, but it also presents a practical, compelling path to combat and overcome envy's deadly undertow. One of the best books on overcoming envy that I have read.

**MARK JOBE**
President of Moody Bible Institute; Senior Pastor, New Life Community Church

We live in a culture saturated with and motivated by envy. Social media and our insatiable drive toward materialism have masked envy as a virtue. By using biblical truth, Fabarez removes that mask to help us see how easily we fall prey to this respectable sin and how the root sin of envy causes deep destruction in our lives. This book is both convicting and refreshing, as Fabarez provides a biblical defense to destroy envious cravings and a biblical offense to pursue godly motivations that bring freedom and life.

**T. DALE JOHNSON JR.**
Executive Director, The Association of Certified Biblical Counselors; Director of Counseling Programs, Midwestern Baptist Theological Seminary

A BIG
PROBLEM
YOU DIDN'T
KNOW
YOU HAD

ENVY

# MIKE FABAREZ

MOODY PUBLISHERS
CHICAGO

Editor: Kevin Mungons
Interior design: Brandi Davis
Cover design: Erik M. Peterson
Cover illustration of emoji courtesy of Iconfinder
Author photo: Donnie Hedrick

Library of Congress Cataloging-in-Publication Data

Names: Fabarez, Michael, 1964- author.
Title: Envy : a big problem you didn't know you had / Mike Fabarez.
Description: Chicago : Moody Publishers, [2023] | Includes bibliographical
    references. | Summary: "Envy. It's insidious. Pervasive. Corrosive. When
    envy is allowed to reside unchecked in our hearts, there are internal,
    relational, and societal costs. Fabarez examines biblical stories of
    envy and invites us to know a kind and gracious Father who calls us to
    identify and assault this enemy"-- Provided by publisher.
Identifiers: LCCN 2023013921 (print) | LCCN 2023013922 (ebook) | ISBN
    9780802431752 | ISBN 9780802473035 (ebook)
Subjects: LCSH: Envy--Religious aspects--Christianity. |
    Jealousy--Religious aspects--Christianity. | Conduct of life. | BISAC:
    RELIGION / Christian Living / Spiritual Growth | RELIGION / Christian
    Living / General
Classification: LCC BV4627.E5 F33 2023  (print) | LCC BV4627.E5 (ebook) |
    DDC 241/.3--dc23/eng/20230705
LC record available at https://lccn.loc.gov/2023013921
LC ebook record available at https://lccn.loc.gov/2023013922

Originally delivered by fleets of horse-drawn wagons, the affordable paperbacks from D. L. Moody's publishing house resourced the church and served everyday people. Now, after more than 125 years of publishing and ministry, Moody Publishers' mission remains the same—even if our delivery systems have changed a bit. For more information on other books (and resources) created from a biblical perspective, go to www.moodypublishers.com or write to:

Moody Publishers
820 N. LaSalle Boulevard
Chicago, IL 60610

1 3 5 7 9 10 8 6 4 2

*Printed in the United States of America*

# CONTENTS

# INTRODUCTION

**The apostle Paul tells Timothy** to "fight the good fight of faith" (1 Tim. 6:12). Near the end of his own life Paul looks back and says, "I have fought the good fight" (2 Tim. 4:7). Elsewhere we are told to "put on the whole armor of God" (Eph. 6:11). These sorts of metaphors continue throughout the New Testament. I wonder, what is it that comes to your mind when you think of your Christian life as a war?

Perhaps you think of the "weapons of warfare" described in 2 Corinthians, which are strategically provided to us as we live in our spiritually hostile culture—biblical weapons, divinely empowered for destroying arguments and lofty opinions that are raised up against the knowledge of God (2 Cor. 10:4–5). Maybe you think of the evangelistic assault that Jesus spoke of as we boldly advance the gospel of grace against "the gates of hell" (Matt. 16:18). Or maybe you're just tired of all this Christian talk of battles, fighting, and warfare, like one author for the HuffPost who was upset with Christians for talking in these militaristic terms. She had had enough of going to church and hearing all the terminology of spiritual conquest and theological combat. She was so resolute and unflinching about the need to soften all religious vocabulary that she wrote "Declaring War on Christian War Metaphors" for a popular news and opinion outlet.[1]

I can certainly appreciate her passion and determined effort to change what she considered to be out of place, but I had to scratch my head at how her zeal was relayed. Her decision to "declare war" on Christian war metaphors seems to make the point as to why they are appropriate and at times even necessary in the first place.

Yes, there is a softer side to our Christian faith—a side where fighting, wrestling, and declaring war won't do. But some things in the Christian life do need to be attacked with the intensity of combat. That may be figurative language; nevertheless at times we must have forceful resolve and take intrepid action. God certainly communicated this with a slew of concerns and jarring analogies. Surely this is why He enlisted these in the Scriptures.

No doubt many of the daunting challenges of the Christian life, like evangelism and apologetics, are going to require the fearlessness of a soldier and the diligence of a military campaign. The many encroaching values, ideals, and ideologies pressing in on us each day require us to armor up to contend for the truth (Jude 3). And many good Christian books are written each year to help us with this ongoing exterior war. This book, however, is not one of them.

We must never forget that the most difficult and personal war we are called to engage in is waged on the *interior* battlefield of our lives. It is the fight of faith that doesn't involve the state university, the White House, or the local school board. It is a wearisome conflict that drags on month after month, and decade after decade. It erupts in costly conflicts today, tomorrow, and the week after next. Sadly, it is a war that we will be waging for the rest of our earthly lives.

God describes our opponent as an inner set of desires and passions that "wage war against your soul" (1 Peter 2:11). The call to arms for every Christian comes with the severity of being ready to "put to death therefore what is earthly in you" (Col. 3:5).

Many of these war motifs are surrounded with helpful lists identifying the evil foot soldiers who are rising up within us and need to be stopped. These embedded enemies of the Christian life are fairly easy to spot. They are the desires of our fallen flesh with familiar insignias like "sexual immorality," "outbursts of anger," and "obscene talk." These are usually identified without difficulty, and when they surface in the fight to be faithful to Christ, they quickly bring regret, shame, and guilt.

However, it is essential for us to be aware that another set of stealthy internal combatants exist. These are so covert, so insidious, and so clandestine that few Christians even realize that they have been assaulted and are under attack. While some sinful desires advance on our hearts with the roar of jet engines and explode in our lives with the deafening impact of 500-pound bombs, other internal enemies are attacking our souls like the camouflaged sniper. They are like well-trained marksmen hiding in the grass, their deadly weapons muted with a silencer. These lethal sharpshooters find their mark and inflict their wounds before we even know what hit us.

Yes, the Christian life is war. And God would have us be ready. We've been warned in God's Word about these covert internal enemies, and we need to be much more vigilant in identifying them than we have been. I have found that one enemy in particular flies incessantly under the radar. It has in my life, and I assume it has in yours as well.

You know where I'm going. The title of this book has clued you in. That one little word represents an injurious threat to your sanctification. It has probably already racked up a multitude of hits in your life. And much of the pain it has caused has been lamented and grieved. But I find we all too often fail to connect the dots. We have not identified the sniper.

As a longtime pastor, I keep a database of the sermons I preach. Not only of the thousands of sermons I have preached to my own congregation here in Southern California, but also of the hundreds of sermons I have preached when I am called to other churches, camps, and conferences. I keep an organized digital list of all the passages of Scripture, and all the related subjects that I address in the pulpit. I take special care with this. Sometimes when a church or an organization asks me to address a particular subject, I'll go back to the database and look at the work I have done on that particular biblical topic. When I was recently asked to examine this particular sin in more detail, I could only find one sermon in thousands where I had directly tackled this ensnaring transgression.

It is time to take a deeper dive into this common but often-overlooked sin. I was convicted to do so while studying Acts 13, where Paul was run out of town and ultimately attacked by a mob. As I was preparing to preach on this passage, I was struck by the fact that the Bible had diagnosed the underlying motive of the leaders for this attempted murder of the apostle. And this incident also very clearly mirrored the underlying motivation of the Jewish leaders when they delivered Christ over to the Romans to be crucified.

What could be more sinister than the divinely identified incentive behind all the opposition, accusations, slander, and these insidious murderous plots? When I stopped to ponder this, I couldn't stop bouncing from one biblical text to the next. All the passages of Scripture filled with conflict, anger, depression, rage, despair, and hostility—all related, in one way or another, to the sin of envy.

From time to time I have moments when things piece together so clearly in my mind, and I realize that something so obvious has been overlooked. And I felt increasingly dumb as I started to remember that I've read about envy many times in old dusty books on pastoral theology. My mind raced back through church history and the vice lists of yesteryear, wherein envy never failed to make an appearance. Envy is one of the "seven deadly sins," as they were often called. Sometimes they were referred to as "capital sins" because they stand as the fountainhead of a thousand lesser sins. These were taught for centuries as the "principal sins," "directors" and "commanders" of so many other transgressions.[2]

If we were to look up what had been standard training for Christians of former generations, we would see familiar sins like pride, greed, lust, and anger. And I've preached a good many sermons that directly address those topics. I've pounded the pulpit, along with so many other pastors, on these notorious transgressions that admittedly lead to a lot of trouble in our inner battle for godliness. Even gluttony and laziness have more recently surfaced in a number of books and sermons and been identified as threats to our Christian growth. But of all the deadly snipers that take aim at today's Christians, I can't think of one who is more cleverly and effectively camouflaged than envy. And I can assure you he is racking up casualties every single day.

It was right after preaching on Acts 13 that I sat through a busy week of appointments, and I felt like every meeting, counseling session, or consultation with other pastors and staffers kept tracing the immediate concern, crisis, or conflict back to envy!

It is my prayer that by a little biblically guided exposure to this threat we can become vigilant, prepared, and equipped to stand strong against the captain of a legion of sins that I'm confident is causing more damage and is a bigger problem in our Christian lives than we currently realize. When we utilize the binoculars of God's Word and are directed by God's Spirit, we will start to see this cunning sharpshooter everywhere. It's time to stop the bleeding and launch an effective counterattack.

At the outset of this short book, we will work to uncover this culprit by exposing it in the lives of many biblical characters, and by so doing arrive at a biblical definition of the problem.

We will then move on to consider the internal costs of letting this vice creep around unchecked in our hearts and minds. We will consider some of the biblical motivations God's Word gives us for routing out this enemy. We will also examine the truth that when a sin like this gets a foothold in our thinking, it will inevitably damage relationships—not just in our families and our inner circle of friends, but also in our churches and even throughout Western civilization. The tentacles of envy have far more relevance to the controversies gripping our society and erupting in our churches than we may think.

We will see God's grace and mercy in His prohibitions, precepts, and strict commands against envy and its related components of coveting and sinful jealousy. We will then start to shape our biblical counterattack by understanding the virtues that can root out and supplant the corrosive effects of this sin. And we will work to safeguard our lives with practices and disciplines prescribed in God's Word, which are most effective when they are aimed against the costly sin of envy.

I trust we will be encouraged by the promises of our Redeemer, who will one day complete His redemptive work in our fallen flesh, restore our rebellious culture, and consign the tempter to his doom. We can find great strength and motivation in the battle as we look to the final victory when Christ is on the throne and our relationships are forever freed from the destructive flare-ups of the formidable foe of envy. May we find what is needed to meet the challenge head-on and make some significant progress beginning today.

Let's get started.

**one**

# EXPOSING ENVY

**Just this morning** I was devotionally reading through the closing chapters of the gospel of John and was again struck by a biblical character with whom I can't help but sympathize. He had a dilemma on his hands. Arguably the greatest one imaginable. He was certainly stuck between a rock and a hard place. Actually, he was wedged between the Cornerstone of God's redemptive work and the hardened angry crowd that was whipped into a violent frenzy.

I'm referring to Pontius Pilate, the Roman governor of Judea. One can imagine how his career would place him between strong competing interests. Trying to govern the first-century religious Jews in the streets of Jerusalem for a powerful Roman emperor who sat ensconced in his palace over 1,400 miles away always came with tensions. Even putting up the obligatory Roman insignias with Caesar's image around the city sparked protests and riots by the Jews.[3]

We are familiar with the scene from Pilate's life that kept him dodging back and forth between doing what he knew was right and appeasing the hostile Jews who were demanding that Jesus be crucified. Even his wife was pushing him to let Jesus go. Unlike the caricature of a Roman official in the arena dispassionately giving the thumbs down to have some poor guy thrown to the lions, Pilate was seriously torn. At moments he was so sympathetic to Christ, and so sincerely leaning in the direction of releasing Jesus, that church traditions are split on whether or not he was a villain and if perhaps he later became an ardent follower of Christ.[4]

Either way, Pilate had good reason to believe the Jewish mob was wrong about Christ. Insightfully, he looked past all the hostility and rhetoric and "perceived that it was out of envy that the chief priests had delivered him up" (Mark 15:10). That may sound like a guess, but it is not meant to be read that way. The Greek New Testament word that is translated "perceived" is the common word for knowing, understanding, or learning something.[5] Pilate, not unfamiliar with the struggle to acquire and maintain power, understood what was going on. He knew that the growing popularity of Christ, the crowds waving palm branches and laying down their cloaks on the road to honor the "Rabbi" as someone great—this was too much limelight for some upstart from Nazareth to steal.

It is astonishing to ponder that the most egregious and unjust act in the Bible—the violent and torturous death of the perfect Son of God—was identified by someone with a front-row seat as motivated by envy. If only the entire citizenry of Judea could have seen it for what it was. If only the Jewish leaders could have looked in the mirror and dealt with the fact that their lives, their teaching, and their leadership just weren't as popular as the Messiah's. If only their self-assessment could have been as clear and perceptive as that of the Roman governor.

## THE MIRROR

I wonder, if we were able to go back in time to interview any of the teenage classmates of Pontius Pilate, or maybe chat with some of his political rivals, how they might rate the governor had we asked if he was the envious type. Would we be surprised to hear that his ambitions in the Roman aristocracy were marked by jealous contentions? Do you think we might hear of some underhanded political maneuvering that included ill-motivated slander or gossip? Do you imagine that we would have a few stories of Pilate stepping on some of his peers because he was envious of their lot? I'm sure we would. But, like most of us, I assume he was largely blind to the frequency of his expressions of envy.

Envy, like all other sins, is so much easier to detect in others than it is in ourselves. If there's one thing God continually points out in His Word, it's that we are naturally inclined to be irritated with others' transgressions long before we ever notice our own. We have a willful and massive blind spot that keeps us feeling just that much better about ourselves. Sadly, our ability to perceive the conniving, competitive, and resentful actions of others qualifies us to be people who, as God puts it, are "without excuse" for our sins. Note the convicting words of the New Testament:

> Therefore you have no excuse, O man, every one of you who judges. For in passing judgment on another you condemn yourself, because you, the judge, practice the very same things. We know that the judgment of God rightly falls on those who practice such things. Do you suppose, O man— you who judge those who practice such things and yet do them yourself—that you will escape the judgment of God? (Rom. 2:1–3)

Recall the acute perception of King David when Nathan relays a story of a man coveting what was his neighbor's and then proceeding to greedily take it for himself. We are told how quickly David's "anger was kindled" and how he blurted out his swift verdict: "the man who has done this deserves to die" (2 Sam. 12:5). And who can forget Nathan's retort that allowed the king to see himself in his own assessment: "You are the man!" (v. 7).

Nathan, by the way, was a prophet. Now if only we had a nearby prophet to point out our double standards. Wait. We do. God's truth is dependably and "actively" sitting on our shelves, and digitally encoded in our phones, waiting to be opened to "pierce" our own souls with conviction over our sin and to dig deep into our lives to discern "the thoughts and intentions of the heart" (Heb. 4:12). After all, we need to see ourselves the way that God does—without double standards. "No creature is hidden from his sight, but all are naked and exposed to the eyes of him to whom we must give account" (Heb. 4:13).

That's a sobering thought. God sees with absolute clarity every secret festering sin problem in our lives. Our desperate need is to see those malignant moral problems as plainly as He does. Until we do, they will inevitably continue to cause damage. The solutions are graciously provided and are available, but before sin can be remedied it must be accurately detected.

God's written Word is the mirror in which we begin to accurately see our own reflection (James 1:23). But it requires that we look "intently." It will require that we look more often. And most importantly for us as Christians, it will require that we look with the resolve to do what it says (v. 22).

Time in God's Word is what we need. We need prayerful, reflective time, considering the whole counsel of God on this topic. And when it comes to the kinds of sins we so often tolerate, the need is urgent. The festering sin of envy is addressed in more passages of Scripture than we might imagine. The problem surfaces often and we can find our own reflection in many narratives and texts of God's truth. We just need to be faithful to begin to look for it.

## WHAT ARE WE LOOKING FOR

You don't have to ask a seventeen-year-old girl what she's looking for as she spends all that time in front of the mirror every morning. She knows. She wants to find all the imperfections and swiftly deal with them. And she has an arsenal laid out on her bathroom counter to work on those disruptive little bumps, blotches, and blemishes.

The malignant disruption we are looking for is called envy. And most of us haven't been all that clued in to what that looks like. So let's examine Jesus' teaching on the matter and see if things won't come into sharp focus, beginning with the example of the day-laborers Christ enlists to illustrate the point.

The story I am referring to is recorded in Matthew 20. The opening line of this parable may raise images of guys in our neighborhoods who line up in the parking lots of hardware stores or local paint shops looking for work. In a town next to mine the city officials have even designed designated day-worker lots and day-laborer centers. Jesus sets the stage in defining envy by describing the verbal agreement of a landowner with a set of day-laborers at the break of dawn. The landowner agrees to give them a "denarius," which was the common wage for a full day of unskilled labor in that first-century culture.

The day-laborers contentedly agree to this fair exchange and head into the fields of the landowner to work in his vineyard. But just like a homeowner heading back to the hardware store mid-morning, the landowner heads back into the marketplace a few hours later and sees more unhired laborers standing around. He calls them to work and says he'll pay them fairly. So off they go to work. A few hours later the owner returns and sees more workers and tells them the same. More day-workers join the team. This happens again mid-afternoon and then just before sundown.

At the end of the day, as the sun sets over the horizon and the crickets start chirping, the foreman is called in by the landowner to line up the workers to pay them. With money bag in hand, the owner first directs the foreman to pay the guys who just showed up an hour before dusk. Surprised and with rising grins on their faces, the workers hold out their hands and receive payment for more than ten times the work they had done.

The workers down the line who had been hired at the crack of dawn also had astonished looks on their faces. But their eyebrows quickly went from raised to furrowed when they received the same day's wage. You can imagine just how zeroed in they must have been, as their chins tucked back to their necks. "What's with those guys?" "What's happening?" "Why are they so special?" "They didn't work a fraction of the time we did!" To quote the words that Jesus put in the mouths of these envious men, "these last worked only one hour, and you made them equal to us who have borne the burden of the day and the scorching heat" (Matt. 20:12).

The landowner's response in Christ's parable doesn't seem to help. "Friend, I am doing you no wrong. Did you not agree with me for a denarius? Take what belongs to you and go" (vv. 13–14). It was hard to argue with that logic. The verbal contract for their labor was kept. It was entered into in good faith, the workers worked, the employer paid what was promised, and all was nice and tidy. Or it would have been—except for the blotches on the human heart. This was the perfect storm to bring to the surface the ugly tendency for fallen creatures to say that "fair" isn't "fair" if it seems "more fair" for someone else.

Then Jesus lowers the boom. He gets to a principle we will need to return to and explore from several angles. His punchline gets to the heart of the problem and helps us understand our English word *envy*.

He says:

> "Take what belongs to you and go. I choose to give to this last worker as I give to you. Am I not allowed to do what I choose with what belongs to me? Or do you begrudge my generosity?" (Matt. 20:14–15)

## THE WORD *ENVY*

What is hidden beneath that last line is the origin of our word *envy*. If you were to examine the original language of the New Testament and see this passage in first-century Greek, you would probably have trouble translating it—even if you studied Koine Greek in college. The phrase is literally read, "Or is your eye evil because I am good?"

My eye? What in the world? Well, it is not a random observation that our eyes do funny stuff when we are in the presence of a person who has it more fair than we do. That furrowed brow and piercing stare is of course the way that our internal begrudging is expressed. Begrudging. There's another word we probably don't use much, but it captures the reason our eyes are looking so evil when someone is the recipient of more "good" from whomever than we are. The word *begrudge* is usually employed when we think of giving. Someone who is resentful about giving is said to be giving begrudgingly. They don't like it.

It makes sense then that the word *grudge* is stuck in the middle of that word. We all know what it means. When we hold a grudge against someone, we feel bitterness and dislike for that person. And I'll bet our faces show it. Our eyes in particular. To give the evil eye, as some of our grandparents called it, is to give a resentful and bitter look to someone who has a blessing or benefit we'd like, and we don't think they should rightly have. Which is why envy is more than just being covetous or jealous (more on that in the next chapter).

Envy goes further than just wanting what someone else has; it is the begrudging, frustrating consternation that *that* person has it. We start to look at them askance. It's what your eye does after working all day for a denarius and seeing the guy down the row get the denarius for only working a fraction of the day. You look at him sideways, casting the kind of glance that your mom used to say would kill someone "if looks could kill."

Envy is frustration. And the vivid way it is depicted is in the universal way we humans cast our eyes on someone we resent because of the blessings, advantages, and opportunities they have, but we don't think they have earned. That is the "evil eye." That is bad, illogical, and sinful resentment leaking out through the look on our faces. That is where the English word *envy* comes from.

The Latin word for staring or looking at someone or something is the word *invidia*. We get the word *video* from the second half of that word. We watch videos. We stare at the screen. The first component of that word "in" in Latin means "on." To look on, to gaze, to give the stink eye to someone in Latin is the origin of the word *envy*. Say *invidia* and *envy* out loud and you'll get it. There's the connection. And while I don't want you to think about staring at videos when you hear the word *envy*, I do want you to remember Christ's descriptive and probing question when

He literally asks, "Is your eye evil because I am good and a generous provider for that person?"

You see what He is getting at. Where's your heart? Are you envious? Do you have resentment and frustration because others have a blessing in their lives that you don't or, as in the laborers' case, you don't think they have earned like you did? Are you angry at someone because you think God has been more generous to them than He has been to you?

## SAUL'S EVIL EYE

Three thousand years ago in Israel, King Saul would have had to confess to all of those things. And why not? A young upstart named David had captured the headlines and the hearts of the Israelites that Saul was called to rule. Sure, David had hurled a well-placed stone between the eyes of the Philistine giant who previously seemed like an unconquerable foe. Yeah, Saul's military commander was so enamored by this performance that he stayed late at the office trying to see how he could add this up-and-coming warrior to his elite team. And who wouldn't be pushed to looking askance at this short, untested, slingshot-toting shepherd teen when all the women in the capital city started cheering, "Saul has struck down his thousands, and David his ten thousands" (1 Sam. 18:7)?

If you were Saul's confidant, I'm sure you'd nod your head in agreement when the king vented his frustration over lunch about what an unearned and unnecessary fuss everyone was making about this kid. To put Saul's emotions in straightforward terms, the Bible says:

And Saul was very angry, and this saying displeased him. He said, "They have ascribed to David ten thousands, and to me they have ascribed thousands, and what more can he have but the kingdom?" And Saul eyed David from that day on. (1 Sam. 18:8–9)

There it is again—the eye. Here is the old expression that captures the meaning of the word *envy*. He eyed David from then on. He would look him up and down and mutter in his mind, "What do they see in this kid? What did he do to deserve all this praise? Do they really think this guy is a better soldier than me? How can someone have so much so quickly? Why does everyone fawn over this runt?"

These are the underlying grudges to which we are all susceptible. It is the recurring sizing up of someone who seems to be getting what we used to have, want to have, or wish we had more of. It is the attitude that involuntarily purses our lips, crinkles our brows, and squints our eyes as our minds mutter, "Why did that guy get the promotion? Why does that woman get all the compliments? Why do their kids get all the breaks?"

Our eye is on that person and our unsettled hearts are resentful, insecure, and frustrated at the injustice and seeming inequity of it all. But unfortunately, that is just the beginning. As I've already mentioned, our spiritual forefathers categorized the sin of envy as a "capital sin" or a "deadly vice" because it inevitably becomes the fuel for a slew of other ungodly things.

### The Envy-Fueled Spears

It is important to note what comes right after the diagnosis of Saul's heart in the book of 1 Samuel. The very next paragraph describes a scene I vividly remember from my days in Sunday school. Of course, our teachers would always have us identify with the young David, victor over Goliath, faithfully serving in Saul's palace, just sitting there discharging his duties as a court harpist. And then, seemingly out of nowhere, my teachers would describe the bearded, crown-wearing monarch erupting in anger and reaching out to hurl his spear across the room at the nimble young David.

As a kid I read that story several times and always thought, "What a terrible and unreasonable thing to have happen to the hero of the story!" But let's be sure to get into Saul's sandals, and at least see ourselves in the story—trying to keep our crown in place while this amateur soldier (and gifted musician) keeps collecting all the piled-on accolades and stealing the increasingly bright spotlight. We should be able to understand and maybe even sympathize with all the pain, frustration, and fear swirling around in the king's heart.

*Fear.* That's the word in 1 Samuel 18:15. Saul was in "fearful awe" of David. Let that one settle in. The more *wowed* he was at the gifts, talents, blessings, and success of David, the more nervous, unsettled, and afraid he felt. And when you feel like that you want it to stop. How can I stop feeling this way? I want them to be less successful. I want them to receive less applause. I want them to get less of the spotlight.

Picking up a spear seems so extreme—especially when I heard the account as a kid in Sunday school, and even now in some ways. But I get it. We want the person we envy to stop it. Stop being who they are. Stop having what they have. Stop taking all the stuff we want for ourselves. I'm sure we have thrown plenty of metaphorical spears at the people we have envied. We have hurled plenty of sharpened criticisms. We have sought to toss a wet blanket over our imagined and feared competitors. We have worked to direct whatever might be within reach to make a feeble and frustrated effort to keep them from being more of what we think they don't deserve to be, and to have less of what we'd like to possess.

Yes, we throw a lot more than just daggers of dirty looks. When we envy, we declare an unspoken war of wishing, hoping, and subtly working to put those undeserving advantaged people in their place. If we were motivated to connect the dots, we could fairly easily detect that secret spear-throwing envy residing in our hearts, just by gauging how we feel when "that person" does get pinned up against the wall. How do we respond when she stumbles? When he loses that important account? When their vacation plans fall apart? When their kids get cut from the varsity team? Do we quietly nod in approval? Is there a sense of perverse satisfaction? Without thinking do we say, "Finally!" or "It was bound to happen!"? Think of how Saul would have felt, and how he would have reacted if it was someone else's spear that wounded David's shoulder on the battlefield. The quiet, or not-so-quiet, joy at watching a rival fall is a sure indicator that envy has been gnawing away at our sound judgment.

That is a big part of the problem with this undetected sin of envy. Even if it is never given full vent in some damaging action, it is always doing damage *in* us. It not only warps our thinking, but it also corrupts our affections. It decimates our peace and degrades our ability to value what is good and steals our opportunities to live truly productive lives. There is so much more to consider, but first let's think back for a moment to the Roman governor who stood between an envious group of Jewish kingpins and the humble and fully composed King of kings.

## PILATE'S DECISION

It was certainly an egregious injustice for Pontius Pilate to hand the innocent Christ over to be murdered on a Roman cross because of the envy of a bunch of insecure scribes and priests. But that is what happened. A cowardly Roman official caved to a fearful set of jealous religious leaders and to the chants of a wishy-washy crowd of angry men and women. No one was without blame. Well, except for the one being beaten, flogged, and hoisted up naked to suffocate on a splintered cross of wood.

That is the good news. That is the gospel. That horrible injustice is the reason God can deal with envious sinners like you and me—justly treating us as though we're not.

The reason for this book is to point out an insidious sin that causes a lot of damage—not just to ourselves, but most importantly to our standing before our Maker. He is the lawgiver and judge (Isa. 33:22; James 4:12). He is the holy rule maker. His rules are good and good for us. And His goodness is so good that He has provided a solution to the portfolio of sins that make us unacceptable before Him.

I do hope this book provides conviction and clarity regarding a particular and far-reaching wrongdoing. But more than that I pray this awareness will always drive us back to the injustice on that Good Friday two thousand years ago. It was good because the triune God dealt with our problem completely and forever. The faultless Father was willing to treat the sinless Son as though He were us. God's justice was settled by that inequitable transaction for those who have been drawn and brought by the Holy Spirit to an honest realization of their sins, and to a sincere repentance that settles their hope in what Christ did that day.

The innocent suffering for the guilty and in place of the guilty— this is what can secure us the forgiveness we desperately need. Though we use the word *innocent* so often in a relative sense, I am speaking in absolute terms. The only reason the innocent suffering of Jesus of Nazareth is a perfectly adequate exchange for the truckload of sin in my life, your life, and an army of others, is because the only innocent one is also the eternal and ever-living One. The infinitely worthy and uncreated Christ, encased in humanity in space and time, is the One who can lay down His holy and righteous life for a multitude of sinful people.

Our awareness of envy, along with every other thought, motive, or action that falls short of God's righteous standards, should drive us to trust in Christ's finished payment for them all. Before we contemplate another aspect of the destructive sins of our lives, and before we prayerfully work to launch a biblically crafted counterattack, may we right now and at every other step along the way thank God that we are enabled to trust in what Jesus accomplished for us the day He was crucified.

The price tag of sin is death, separation, and expulsion from God and His blessings, but the completed work of Christ in earning our forgiveness is the means by which we can be exonerated. We can be freed from guilt. Not just feeling guilty, but being guilty. Because He has lived in our place and died in our place, we can have an actual and full discharge of our criminal sentence. We can trust in a Redeemer who reversed the wages of sin and proved it by walking out of a dark, dank, and ghastly grave.

Fighting sin in our lives is important. But knowing that our sins are forgiven is of ultimate importance. Let's identify the problem of envy and all the ensuing mess that it causes. Let's fight temptation and shore up the weak points with the Spirit's wisdom and by the Spirit's empowerment. But let's do it as forgiven people. Let's attack envy as Christians who know and fully trust in the fact that the biggest fight was won the day Pilate sinfully capitulated to the angry mob and the Father saw us in the words, "It is finished" (John 19:30).

two

# THE INTERNAL COSTS OF ENVY

**Here in California,** just about every office, store, restaurant, bank, and amusement park has a warning sign affixed next to the entrance that tells me that the place I am entering has chemicals that are "known to the state to cause cancer." If you are familiar with the history of California politics, these omnipresent Proposition 65 signs are the result of the 1980s environmental activism of Jane Fonda and Tom Hayden. Their decades-old alarm has now required warning signs for a growing list of close to one thousand substances. Whether you're buying a pillow or a cup of coffee, if you are in my home state, you have been warned.

It's not hard to guess what these pervasive warnings have done. Besides being the catalyst for countless lawsuits, they have anesthetized the average consumer who views them with the same interest as the speed-rolled, small-font credits at the end of the movies they watch—they ignore them. The words aren't shouted by the doorman and the signs aren't illuminated with flashing lights. For most of us they are just nicely formatted words, neatly arranged on the wall, causing little to no concern as we get to the business of shopping, banking, or taking the kids on the Ferris wheel.

You'd have to admit that some of God's biblical warnings seem to have built-in strobe lights, and others ring in our ears like the volume is turned up all the way to ten. These are scriptural passages about egregious sins and their destructive consequences, which make us gulp and bring an immediate sense of fear and conviction. They are easy to identify, and they smack our consciences hard. But the sins we are attempting to diagnose in this book are more like those Prop 65 signs. We likely scroll right past them when we read our Bibles. True, the font size of the verses that warn and prohibit envy and coveting is the same as those about adultery and murder, but our eyes and hearts just don't see them the same. The former don't have the unsettling resonance they deserve.

## READING THREE-DIMENSIONALLY

The reason certain sins seem so much more serious than others is because we can quickly imagine their devastating impact. We don't have to stretch to envision the gaping loss left if we were to have a family member brutally murdered by some violent thug. It does not take hours to consider the wreckage were your family to be torn apart by someone's adulterous conquests. But to read that we are not to envy, well, no sudden images of personal collapse or relational debris come to mind.

Formulating an accurate sense of the sin of envy will require not only a broad reading of Scripture, but also a thoughtful consideration of the Bible's narrative. We will need the breadth of God's Word and the depth of our contemplation to see how the historical accounts of the lives of numerous biblical characters were affected by this sin. In surveying Genesis to Revelation we may not think that God warns often of envy, but the story of envy's contagion is on just about every other page.

This observation was made by the students of the Bible who have gone before us. Some of the notable teachers of God's people have sounded the alarm with flashing lights, bells, and whistles. Consider Augustine, who, at the turn of the fifth century, cautioned Christians that envy was the diabolical sin—as in the original sin of Satan. "And that is pride, the beginning of all sin; and the beginning of the pride of man is to fall off from God. The devil added malevolent envy to his pride when he persuaded man to share his pride."[6]

About three hundred years ago, the Rev. William Law, who had a great influence on George Whitefield and John Wesley, put all his disciples on notice that the evil of envy is "the most ungenerous, base, and wicked passion that can enter the heart of man."[7]

Back in the time of Augustine, John Chrysostom was in Constantinople warning his congregation with a sermon about envy's ability to take root in one's soul. He preached it in such a way that I can safely say it would most definitely get your attention, had you been sitting there that Sunday:

> To what then is one to compare a soul of this kind? to what viper? to what asp? to what cankerworm? to what scorpion? since there is nothing so accursed or so pernicious as a soul of this sort. For it is this, it is this, that hath subverted the Churches, this that hath gendered the heresies, this it was that armed a brother's hand, and made his right hand to be dipped in the blood of the righteous . . .[8]

Before we consider that first human hand dipped in blood, we should look even further back to the very first sin that Cyprian, the third-century pastor, diagnosed in the original sinner himself—Satan:

> When he beheld man made in the image of God, broke
> forth into jealousy with malevolent envy—not hurling down
> another by the instinct of his jealousy before he himself was
> first hurled down by jealousy, captive before he takes captive,
> ruined before he ruins others. . . . How great an evil is that,
> beloved brethren, whereby an angel fell, whereby that lofty
> and illustrious grandeur could be defrauded and overthrown,
> whereby he who deceived was himself deceived! Thenceforth
> envy rages on earth. . . . They who are on his side imitate him.[9]

There's no way to read statements like that from church history and not begin to think that our spiritual forefathers considered the implications of the biblical narratives much more deeply. The vast magnitude of the sin of envy, its potential impact, and its association with God's ultimate enemy were well summarized by the intertestamental Book of Wisdom, which reminded its readers: "through the envy of the devil, death entered the world."[10]

## HUMANITY'S FIRST MURDER

The Bible doesn't hesitate to connect our internal temptation of envy to Satan's ominous work. The apostle John listed Cain's murder of Abel as a cautionary example of what might be brooding in our own hearts: "We should not be like Cain, who was of the evil one . . ." (1 John 3:12). The sin he highlights next as the underlying fuel—which might currently be luring you or me into even greater sins—can rightly be said to be in league with the devil. That's a big statement.

It's time for us as Christians to take such forthright statements at face value. Few things could be more insidious. It's hard to imagine a more explosive fuel than one that could unleash the most appalling sins like the problem Cain had festering inside him regarding his brother Abel.

The Bible goes on to describe the motivation for that first homicide with the words, "Because his own deeds were evil and his brother's righteous" (v. 12b). Let's recall the scene.

> In the course of time Cain brought to the LORD an offering of the fruit of the ground, and Abel also brought of the firstborn of his flock and of their fat portions. And the LORD had regard for Abel and his offering, but for Cain and his offering he had no regard. So Cain was very angry, and his face fell. The LORD said to Cain, "Why are you angry, and why has your face fallen? If you do well, will you not be accepted? And if you do not do well, sin is crouching at the door. Its desire is contrary to you, but you must rule over it." (Gen. 4:3–7)

The apostle John's authoritative commentary is helpful. Whatever was wrong with the offering, which is always a curious question, it was something that God considered "evil." The offering was rejected because Cain's heart, life, actions, or whatever else was sinful. A sacrificial offering, wherever it might come from, wasn't going to fix this problem. At that point, repentance and trust in God's mercy was required. Instead, the temptation shifted from whatever the initial problem was to the problem of seeing his brother do well and being received by God.

In whatever way God demonstrated the "favor" upon Abel and his offering, it was clear to Cain that he didn't have it. The blessing, peace, joy, or visible demonstration of the Lord's thumbs-up drove Cain crazy. Notice how God directs him. "Do well." "Get it together!" "Repent and make things right with me." It was as though God was saying, "This is about you and Me, not you and him. Forget what's going on over there, let's have you get things right and move forward in your own life." But Cain couldn't handle it. Who knows what thousands of thoughts ran through Cain's brain as his hostility toward his brother grew. "Why him? Why not me? It's not fair. It's not right. How can he be doing so much better than me?"

Cain spiraled down into a compounding and multiplied set of horizontal comparisons. His "fallen face" and bad attitude took his eyes off the productive plan to reorder his life before the only One who ultimately mattered—the God who was his Judge as well as his gracious and forgiving Redeemer. Acceptance and personal progress were potentially in his future, but instead, a much more powerful sin was busy getting its hooks in his heart. It was "crouching at the door" and he had to fight it. But I would confidently guess he wasn't busy looking that sin in the eyes. Instead, he was busy fixating on the contented eyes of his brother.

The next verse in Genesis 4 matter-of-factly unfolds: "Cain rose up against his brother Abel and killed him" (v. 8). Yikes! Talk about an explosive and dominating sin—not the murder, but the motive. Of course the sin is horrific. Killing someone with malice aforethought is a horrendous, sinful act of violence, but let us soak in the reason *why*. What kind of preceding violence was envy wreaking on the interior of Cain's life? Hour after hour and day after day, his hostility was ramping up and all he could think about was tearing down the one who had what he didn't have.

## UNTANGLING JEALOUSY, COVETING, AND ENVY

If you think about Cain's interior life on the days leading up to the murder, it's not hard to imagine that it was anything but tranquil.

We envision his mind being pushed and pulled by all sorts of strong, disruptive, turbulent thoughts and emotions. It might be good to try to sort them out and identify them biblically. It will provide us another step in understanding the entangled mess from which God would like to set us free.

Our Creator, the One who knows us best, has diagnosed three distinguishable but often intertwined experiences that we have all privately been wrestling with for as long as we can remember. I say *wrestling* because they are all intruders that get in the way of our feelings of peace, tranquility, and joy. We like those pleasant feelings of calm. We don't like them being upended by uninvited antagonists—especially the kind that keep our minds spinning and our stomachs churning.

## Jealousy

All of these unpleasant realities are indicators that something is wrong. Sometimes, as in the case of jealousy, it can indicate that something is wrong with someone else. There is clearly a time for alarm bells to go off in our hearts when someone who should be rightly and uniquely loyal, loving, and linked to us is straining that link by giving their love and loyalty elsewhere.

The agonizing heartache and unsettling indignation of a broken marriage vow or a cheating girlfriend are examples of appropriate feelings of intensely wanting something we don't currently have. We know that these feelings are appropriate, because the God of the universe reveals Himself to be perfectly holy and rightly jealous. He clearly does not experience the feelings precisely the way we do, but the sinless triune God tells us as clearly as possible in Exodus 34:14, "You shall worship no other god, for the LORD, whose name is Jealous, is a jealous God." What a way to put it! "My name is Jealous." It couldn't be more definitive. And the context in the beginning of the verse helps us understand that there is obviously nothing wrong with Him, but only with the idolators.

All of humanity should recognize God and be devoted to Him— the only God. The God who created, sustains, and grants each of them life and breath and every daily provision. When they enthrone something or someone other than God in the place of God, God says He will express and act from His holy attribute of jealousy.

The problem with our jealousy is that we are so often jealous about something or someone when we have no right to be. We cannot be jealous that one friend gives more honor or attention to another friend who just happens to not be "us." We often make imaginary and misguided claims in our own hearts about positions, possessions, or people not rightly or uniquely ours. This is when our hearts must be called out for being territorial, controlling, and clingy, because having those roles, relationships, and riches is based solely on our selfish need to feel better in having them. When this unjustified second sort of jealousy is present in our lives, it can be said to have a similarity with the sins of coveting and envy.

### Coveting

Unlike jealousy, the sin of coveting always indicates there is something wrong in us, not in someone else. It is sometimes provoked when I consider someone else, but only because that someone possesses the person, place, or thing my heart has decided it cannot be happy without. And that is a decision that is always wrong. It is the antithesis of contentment—the godly virtue every Christian must seek to take hold of. A genuine and growing relationship with Christ is the open secret to this interior satisfaction that Paul says is possible in "whatever situation" and "in any and every circumstance," whether "facing plenty" or "hunger," having "abundance" or "need" (Phil. 4:11–12).

Coveting is such a fundamental sin that it was embedded by the Lord as the tenth commandment—one that comes with more examples than any of the other nine. Consider again the all-encompassing words of Exodus 20:17, "You shall not covet your neighbor's house; you shall not covet your neighbor's wife, or his male servant, or his female servant, or his ox, or his donkey, or anything that is your neighbor's."

It is easy to identify this feeling, especially if your neighbor is doing better than you. And certainly, someone in your neighborhood is. His car is hard to ignore. Noticing hurts. Why? Because he's driving what you want. *Coveting* is the word for *really* wanting something badly. Whether it's a house or a spouse, cars or cash. It's something you crave. As Albert Mohler unpretentiously put it, coveting is all about hankering, people hankering after things they want.[11] Maybe not the synonym you would expect from the learned Dr. Mohler, but it certainly captures the nuance of the problem. Coveting is more than merely wanting something, pursuing someone, or aspiring to some position; it is deeper than that. It crosses into an obsessive craving and unquenchable thirst to just "having to have" the object of our desire. It leads some to pine away in self-pity, and others to fanatically chase after their preoccupation.

Either way, coveting is a fixation to capture what we do not have. It is based on the addictive illusion that if we just have the object of our desire, we will be satisfied. But as poets have written and rock stars have sung, the satisfaction doesn't dawn. The fulfillment doesn't last. The mirage of arriving is never realized.

Solomon reflects upon his life of hankering and asks, "What has a man from all the toil and striving of heart with which he toils beneath the sun? For all his days are full of sorrow, and his work is a vexation. Even in the night his heart does not rest. This also is vanity" (Eccl. 2:22–23).

## Envy

Even our initial consideration of envy is enough to enable us to see how inappropriate jealousy and the discontented cravings of coveting can overlap with envy. They are distinct, but often interlaced. But worse than either, envy takes things a sinful step further. Whether I am hurt over not having what I feel entitled to, or I fixate on what I'm convinced would make me happy, these unpleasant thoughts and feelings escalate after simmering in my heart until my sense of deprivation leads me to resent the people who have what I want. And not just any people, usually it's the person right in front of me.

As Tilly Dillehay succinctly states, "Envy thrives among peers."[12] I don't resent the guy on YouTube driving the truck I just have to have or living in the man cave I've always wanted. It's the coworker, the guy in my small group, my brother-in-law, or the neighbor I wave at every morning on my way to work. When they have what I crave, and they get to experience what I've dreamed of, then I start looking at them with disdain.

Envy shifts the focus to the person. It drives me to ruminate about how that person is less deserving, less worthy, or just less. It leads me to desire that they not only do without the privileges and possessions I want, but if that hurts them—that is fine too. Think of how undetected and unchecked envy compounds the problem in me. The problem is not them. Actually, in some other universe I might even be happy that my brother, or my brother in Christ, had the things that I know all too well are gifts, blessings, and honors. But sadly, I am secretly cursing the people I am called to rejoice with when they are blessed. And even more appalling, I would take pleasure in their pain.

God has stern words for the fruit of envy. Consider this barrage of conviction from our Maker:

Whoever despises his neighbor is a sinner. (Prov. 14:21a)

But do not gloat over the day of your brother in the day of his misfortune . . . do not boast in the day of distress . . . do not gloat over his disaster in the day of his calamity. (Obad. 12–13a)

Let not your heart be glad when he stumbles, lest the LORD see it and be displeased. (Prov. 24:17b–18a)

He who is glad at calamity will not go unpunished. (Prov. 17:5b)

God obviously wants something different for us. Something better. As challenging as it may be in our fallen world, God's Spirit wants to enable you and me to truly love our neighbor, to sincerely rejoice in the advantages of others, and to find contented satisfaction in our less-than-perfect lives. That's what this book is all about. But we can't get there if we don't see the seriousness of the problem and admit that we have it—to one degree or another.

## ASSESSING MOTIVES

Accurately detecting why we do what we do is never easy. The Bible tells us that even the smartest among us struggle to perceive themselves rightly (Rom. 2:1). Self-analysis is by definition subjective. We need the light of biblical truth to inject some objectivity into the understanding of our own internal motivations. But I hope that even at this point of the book you have already been able to trace some of your previously inexplicable resentment, sadness, frustration, or discontentment to the sinful root of envy.

I pray that it is already somewhat easier after a little reflection and self-appraisal to see that the bitterness toward your more successful or more attractive friend is fueled and sustained by the envy that resides in your heart. Perhaps a little light on this subject has helped you to see that your snarky comments about the neighbor kid's college scholarship, or the unexpected internal pain of just scrolling through the vacation photos of the woman at church with the perfect teeth, is another indicator that the vicious evil of envy has set up shop in your soul.

And if you are a guy, let me speak directly to you for a minute. I have heard some men say that envy is a "women" problem. They say, "I don't really envy others; I just go about my daily work." I trust that if you have read this far, you know better. But hearing that statement just this week reminded me of Solomon's insightful assessment of what he diagnosed in his male-dominated workforce. God's Spirit utilized him to write, "Then I saw that all toil and all skill in work come from a man's envy of his neighbor. This also is vanity and a striving after wind" (Eccl. 4:4). This sweeping statement cannot be divorced from the biblical affirmation that work itself is a pre-fall gift of God. In other words, while all work after Genesis 3 is certainly infected by the consequences of sin, skill and toil are necessary assignments for everybody, and can be engaged in without envy. Solomon's broad appraisal of men's motives speaks to the pervasive societal problem that plagues hearts—while not without exception, certainly "all" without distinction.

Most workers, craftsmen, scholars, artisans, and pastors pursue their daily work with rivalrous attention to their colleagues, competitors, and challengers. It may be harder to detect when you are getting the job done, pleasing your boss, and sensing job security. But God wants us to consider that sin might be motivating more of what we do than we might first imagine. Think about it. From picking a college, a major, or a profession, every human is prone to do so with influences from some deep-seated and rarely acknowledged jealousy, covetousness, and yes, even envy. This verse from Ecclesiastes helps us see that people from every walk of life tend to make business decisions, craft agenda items, put together marketing plans, and set sales goals with an envious eye on the other guy.

Consider the words of Groucho Marx, of all people. He was the shrewd, cosmopolitan comedian and movie star of early films. In his autobiography he laid aside his slapstick to reflect on the problem that Solomon so clearly articulated. Groucho laments,

> It is very disconcerting for a comic to sit in a dressing room and listen to another comedian kill the audience with laughter. "Bravo" is a wonderful word when shouted at you, but a most disturbing accolade when bestowed upon a competitor. . . . Having been only in the theatrical profession, I don't know how people in other walks of life react to success and failure. But I'm sure you'll find that a wide streak of envy is part of almost everyone's make-up. . . . I will probably be stoned for the following, but it's my contention that the laying of a large-sized theatrical egg on Broadway brings joy and relief to a substantial section of the entertainment world. . . . Permanent success in show business is unforgivable.[13]

Of course, the same is true of women in every field of work. But I make this quick parenthetical point for the man who misses the big envy problem in his own life because he is busy thinking that envy is always about his wife resenting her friend with the better body. Oh, and by the way, I've been to the gym, and I know body envy is driving the reps of both men and women alike.

## TIME TO CONFESS

The second half of Proverbs 14:30 tells us that "envy makes the bones rot." Let's start the process of being done with that. Who wouldn't want to be? Even secular academics have quipped, "Of the seven deadly sins, only envy is no fun at all."[14] So, with God's help, let's resolve to get this behind us. Breaking envy's grip on us, along with all its associated damage, will take several steps, a few new godly habits, and a bit more assessment on a larger scale, but at this point, let's take responsibility for what we see is taking place in ourselves. The first step in eradicating any sinful vice in our lives is admitting we have it—no more excuses.

The problem of envy is like a pebble in our shoe. People may not see it. And we may not see it directly. But we can feel it. It is causing pain. It is affecting our gait. If it has been there long enough it has caused problems for our ankles, knees, hips, and back. People may not know what our problem is, but they know we are not walking quite right. Before we stoop down to start to deal with the problem, we've got to know it's there. But unfortunately, unlike a pebble that we have the dexterity and power to get to and extract, sinful problems of the heart require God's abilities. This is what makes Christian confession so much more than non-Christian acknowledgment of having a problem. As Christians we know that the problem is more than just trouble for us, it is an offense to God. We know we can't just say, "Let's forget that ever happened"—we need forgiveness and pardon. And we know the ability to do better next time is not something we can just muscle up and do (though it will certainly require all of our spiritual muscles!). We need God. We need His grace and His provision. We need His Spirit and His enablement.

So let us confess our sins, specifically, not just the symptoms, but the root causes. Let's not just agree with God that it was wrong to say what we said, or be as unloving as we were, but let us tell Him we know that we have nursed the secret sin of envy. And don't say, "Well, until today I didn't know." Even if that is true, the day we know is the day we must confess. Whether you are a plumber or a preacher, a mathematician or a mom, tell God you see the problem and you know you have not been an innocent bystander. Reach out for His merciful forgiveness. Let's be grateful that along with King David we can confidently say:

I acknowledged my sin to you,
    and I did not cover my iniquity;
I said, "I will confess my transgressions to the LORD,"
    and you forgave the iniquity of my sin.
(Ps. 32:5)

three

# THE RELATIONAL COSTS OF ENVY

**A nice line of trees** separates our driveway from my neighbor's. They look great. My wife likes them. But they are causing me trouble. Lots of trouble. I guess to be specific, it's not the trees causing me so many problems, but the secret and powerful things underneath them—to which I had never really given any thought. That is, at least until these long and growing wooden tentacles began to break up my driveway. And my neighbor's driveway. And his water main. And the drains running from my house out to the curb. And the brick wall between my house and the neighbor's house on the other side.

These tentacles are not like our infamous California earthquakes, which do all their damage at one time. The nefarious roots of these beautiful trees wreak havoc on my bank account—an expensive episode one year, and another costly episode the next. They are my trees. They are clearly on my side of the property line.

I admired them when the realtor showed us the house seventeen years ago. But little did I know what came with them. I learned within a few years that they paid no attention to the property line. They loved making trouble for me with my neighbors. It was one thing when they first busted up my own garden drainage pipe, but it was a whole new ballgame when my neighbor came over with an estimate to have a contractor haul off his broken driveway and re-pour the whole thing with new concrete.

Selfishly, on a random day off, I would like to have said, "Hey, that's your driveway, not mine—fix it yourself!" But I knew better. Those roots are from my trees. Any simple investigation could prove that. I also quickly learned that laws dealing with such matters have been on the books in our state since 1872 (section 833 of the civil code, if you must know), and I am fully responsible for the transgressive roots of the trees my wife loves so much.

## THE CLANDESTINE DESTROYER

To know that envy disrupts the peace, contentment, and joy that God would otherwise grant to our internal life is bad enough, but even worse is the fact that if envy is not detected, dug up, and thrown out it will inevitably inflict some serious relational damage on the people we are walking next to in life. Cain and Abel might express the most extreme example of one person literally killing another on account of envy, but we can be sure that quite a few of our past relationships have been "killed" for the same reason. We may blame the boneyard of past friendships on all sorts of things, but in reality the unseen destroyer in many cases can be traced back to the sin of envy.

Consider some of the symptomatic expressions that seep out from unrepentant envy. Let's start with a fairly broad term that we are more likely to identify as a reason a relationship should end, while we continue to remain ignorant of the underlying cause. The word God uses is *hatred*. When asked why we don't want to hang out with that person anymore, or why we'd rather not go to the game with him, or go to her dinner party, we might say, "I just don't like that person."

"But why?" our spouse might ask.

"I just really don't like that guy," we blurt out. That will usually end the discussion and change our weekend plans, but "hatred" really isn't the reason. In many cases, it is only a manifestation of the true problem.

Here's how God's Word describes the mess: "For we ourselves were . . . passing our days in malice and envy, hated by others and hating one another" (Titus 3:3). In that sentence the word *envy* sits surrounded by the effects that it has on the way we relate to each other. *Malice* may not be a word we use every day, but I remember memorizing the Greek word from which it is translated. It was easy for me to remember, because to me it always sounded like the thing it was—an onomatopoeia in my mind. The Greek word is *kakia*! It reminded me of the words *yucky* or *icky*. This word carries the idea of junk that is bad. It refers to things that are evil or harmful. It is even translated "trouble" in the familiar passage where Jesus said each day has enough *kakia* of its own (Matt. 6:34). That's for sure. Every day has some bad stuff in it. The yucky stuff.

The words on the other side of "envy" in Titus 3:3 are super familiar—"hated" and "hating." But in the original language of this text, they translate two different words. The first word translated "hated" is only used once in the Bible. Outside of the Bible, in other early Greek writings, it refers to people who are considered despicable, abominable, or disgusting.[15] These are people we don't like— people we *really* don't like! The other word translated "hating" is roughly synonymous, and a term used commonly throughout the New Testament for a sense of disfavor and disregard of another person. It certainly carries with it the strong disdain that leads us to announce, "I just can't stand her!"

At the core of these terrible things is our familiar word envy— resentment and bitterness toward someone because they get to enjoy and experience the blessings we crave. Our unrestrained desires for their blessings and privileges grow into an intense irritation and our secret wish for their pain, loss, or embarrassment. When envy gets in between me and that person it results in bad and hateful words, actions, and innuendos that do nothing but ensure the destruction of whatever relationship might be left. And that is a big deal. Bigger than we'd like to think.

God has told us,

Whoever says he is in the light and hates his brother is still in darkness. Whoever loves his brother abides in the light, and in him there is no cause for stumbling. But whoever hates his brother is in the darkness and walks in the darkness, and does not know where he is going, because the darkness has blinded his eyes. (1 John 2:9–11)

"God, I do love my brothers and sisters," we say, "maybe not all of them, but the ones I like—I love." We may rationalize these kinds of sins with nonsensical ideas like that, but let's think for a moment and consider standing before Christ when He evaluates our lives and "laying down" that line. It won't fly. We wouldn't dare attempt to utter it. All the contemporary sentimental Christian music notwithstanding, we won't be dancing and frolicking with Jesus, at least not before we, as His humble and unworthy servants, stand before Him for our evaluation—the evaluation that carefully considers how we have kept His Word and what things motivated our hearts (1 Cor. 4:5). That's a sobering thought, but one that is supposed to snap us to attention and have us take His Word and our sins seriously.

This, by the way, is not a reference to a prelude of some sort of purgatory where we will go so we can burn off our sins for a specified period of time.[16] It is rather the judgment for rewards that will certainly come with some tears and pain of lost opportunities, due in large part to our skill of rationalizing our sins. Not only does 1 Corinthians 3:11–15 speak clearly to this future reality for Christians, but Romans 14:10 puts it in the context of our relationships—"Why do you pass judgment on your brother? Or you, why do you despise your brother? For we will all stand before the judgment seat of God." Talk about snapping us to attention! In the words of 1 Peter 1:17, "And if you call on him as Father who judges impartially according to each one's deeds, conduct yourselves with fear throughout the time of your exile."

In the time that remains of our "exile" on this sinful planet, it won't be easy or comfortable to regularly monitor our hearts for impulses of disdain, bitterness, or resentment toward the more gifted, more beautiful, or more advantaged, but we must. Leading a circumspect life is essential for those of us who know the truth. We have to be vigilant and on guard against the ugly roots of envy that threaten to break up our connections with one another.

## MADE FOR RELATIONSHIPS

At times I've been tempted, in my vigilance and amid grief over my own bitterness toward others, to just withdraw. I've stroked my chin and wondered if the Desert Fathers of church history, back in the third and fourth centuries, were onto something. Maybe an emotional retreat for the remainder of my "exile" to a relational desert without all this "Christian communal stuff" is the way to go. I could avoid all the bitterness, frustration, and temptation to envy by being a twenty-first century-monk who keeps everyone at arm's length.

Nope.

I will go so far as to say that the whole monastic enterprise of the religious hermits took a decent idea too far. I get the value of "retreats" and "alone time." Jesus did it for hours at a time, and once even for over a month (Mark 1:35–37; Matt. 4:1–2). But the predominant example of Christ, who was in close, intertwined human relationships, as well as the required outworking and significance of all the New Testament "one another" commands, forces me to conclude that physical or relational hermithood is not allowed.

God made us all for relationship—married or single, father of seven or widowed empty-nester. God meant it when He said it's not good for man to be alone (Gen. 2:18). Adam had God, but he was designed for friendships, partnerships, and comradery. Jesus was God and had a better, more gratifying spiritual relationship with God the Father than we could ever imagine, and yet He lived, traveled, and leaned on a circle of twelve guys and had a network of men and women He was deeply devoted to, as well as a team of seventy that He engaged in ministry with. He didn't withdraw. He wasn't distant. He didn't say that close human relationships aren't worth the pain, heartache, or temptation.

I wouldn't want to speculate as to how exactly envy might have been a temptation for Christ (though I can imagine living life with close friends who would never have to suffer the Father's wrath for sins on the cross would certainly not be easy), but I do know that He is not "unable to sympathize with our weaknesses, but [is] one who in every respect has been tempted as we are, yet without sin" (Heb. 4:15). Jesus was harassed by temptation, but He chose not to isolate. We can't isolate either.

God knows the hazards and liabilities of getting to know people well. He is aware that you will discover things in your friends' lives that you desperately want. He is sure you will have friends, relatives, and coworkers who have been given things in life that have been taken away from you. The Lord is not blind to the fact that in truly caring, loving, and praying for others you will be tempted to covet, because you will see the disparity in various categories of life—between their prosperity and your deprivation. He knows you will be tempted to say, "Why should I be praying for another blessing or victory for little Ms. I-Have-Everything-I-Want?" Even so, God expects you to lean into relationships and not shy away from them. God would rather you read a Christian book like this and begin to quell the waves of resentment and discontent in your life, than have you run away from the circle of people in which He has placed you.

## FALSE ADVERTISING

I was recently staying in a hotel that didn't seem all that fancy, but the restaurant on the first floor was certainly trying. Being raised as a latchkey kid from Long Beach and having my taste buds conditioned by hot dogs and Top Ramen, I'm not an exotic eater. Ask anyone who knows me. They've learned not to invite me over for fancy foods. I have twelve things I like, and I have no interest in venturing beyond them. Anyway, this restaurant had a one-page menu with a list of fancy-sounding items, none of which I could envision. I began to wish for pictures next to each item. That would have helped. But then again, maybe it wouldn't. I'm sure we have all been to eateries that spent more money on the menu photoshoot than on the kitchen equipment. You know what I mean. The plate comes out and you want the menu back to try to find a resemblance.

People's lives are much the same. Especially in the modern era. And I mean the modern, modern era—like in the last ten or fifteen years. The problem of knowing if Grandma's doodied-up, sweet-talking friend from church is all she presented herself to be has become a lot harder since she got a social media account. And people of Grandma's age are not half as good at presenting their best public selves as their grandchildren are—who know exactly what to post, when to post, and what filters to use.

The celebrated social psychologist Jonathan Haidt proves that even an atheist can see all the damage done by runaway envy that is fueled by the self-presentation and personal false advertising of social media. His interviewer in a 2022 *Wall Street Journal* article quotes his lament:

"You post your perfect life, and then you flip through the photos of other girls who have a more perfect life, and you feel depressed." He calls this phenomenon "compare and despair" and says: "It seems social because you're communicating with people. But it's performative."[17]

"Compare and despair." That's a pithy and accurate commentary on where we're at. And it also happens to be the core component of the sin of envy. The temptation to envy in a performative world was bad enough when we worked in the same office with someone or participated in the same small group Bible study, but now we go home and see a whole new level of choreographed performance. Your buddy stands there in all his staged vacation photos, you see the retouched and retaken pictures of him and his wife in their softly lit embrace on date night, and watch the video of his kid scoring the game-winning touchdown. Even his dog seems to smile for the camera.

Sadly, so much of our envy is foolishly amplified because we begin to believe all the false advertising of what we think other people's lives are like. Without any resentment-stoked satisfaction, I can tell you from my vantage point as a longtime pastor in the same congregation, that what you see on Sundays or even Wednesday nights is often far from the reality of the members' messy and pained lives. From the church counseling offices, I can tell you that some of the most venomous and embattled marriages keep up with a regular flow of the sweetest and most affectionate arm-in-arm profile pictures, and a barrage of loving public compliments. Kids and parents who are at each other's throats can be great at posting the most beautiful and poised family photos—where everyone is wearing matching white shirts and rolled up jeans while their feet are gently washed by the waves at the beach. You can scroll and stare at "gratified and fulfilled lives" that don't exist. You can pine away or begin to hope that the Smiths fall into the ocean, but what you're envying is rarely the reality.

When we believe the myth of the perfect marriage, or the most amazing job, or the idyllic neighborhood, and buy into the exaggerations of people who say they have them, it makes it all that much more difficult to stop comparing and despairing. But we must. And it is a little bit easier when we know that much of what we envy or resent is just a façade.

Consider your own life for a minute. First spend a good chunk of time in the mirror of God's Word and allow the sharp edges of God's written revelation to cut deep into your own conscience (James 1:22–27; Heb. 4:12–13). Then think for a minute about the people who may envy you. Imagine what they believe about all they admire about you. Think of how strong, patient, selfless, or forgiving you are. How would you feel to know they are struck with sorrow that they don't have it all together like you? Imagine if they have growing resentment for you because, after all, you are just so amazing. You get the point. Only Jesus was all He was cracked up to be. The rest of us have a chasm of various miles between the "me" people envy, and the "me" that really exists. And yet relationships are strained, damaged, and some are even obliterated because of the festering evil of envy.

## THE COSMIC BATTLE

It may be a challenge to consider that my strained relationships and deteriorating friendships are a strategic part of a battle between heaven and hell, but that is the profound truth. Remember the description in 1 John 3:12 where Cain, who was embroiled in envy toward his brother, was said to be "of the evil one" and so murdered his brother Abel. The demise of this first sibling relationship is tied to Satan himself. As Jesus stated in describing the highest-ranking enemy of God, he comes "only to steal and kill and destroy" (John 10:10). The chief angelic destroyer has set his sights not only on separating us from God, but also on separating us from each other. And that makes sense. If Jesus says that nothing is more important than that we love God with all of our heart, and then adds that we are also to love our neighbor as ourselves, then certainly the enemy of Christ is going to be dead set on undoing both. God has affirmed "how good and pleasant it is when brothers dwell in unity" (Ps. 133:1). So we can be sure that Satan is actively dispatching his demonic henchmen to disrupt the relationships we have with one another. And it is ominous to consider that the very first tool he used in destroying human fraternity was the crowbar of envy.

In my lectures on the topic of angels and demons, I have often summarized that promoting relational conflict among us and doing his best to keep us apart are among the top priorities of God's archenemy. Knowing the enemy's strategy in this regard might do us good in working hard to fight his temptations.

The spiritual battle "in heavenly places," as Ephesians 6:12 calls it, is always on the cusp of breaking out into relational battles here on earth. And yes, even in the most tightly knit circles within the church. Consider the warning of God to the young pastor Timothy when he is told, "Have nothing to do with foolish, ignorant controversies; you know that they breed quarrels" (2 Tim. 2:23). The passage goes so far as to say that there are emissaries for evil inside of the church who have been caught up in "the snare of the devil, after having being captured by him to do his will" (v. 26). The one Jesus said is prowling around to steal, kill, and destroy is attempting to create friction, conflict, and destruction, and so often he uses his favorite weapon of envy, which most people give little or no thought to these days.

## HARD SOLUTIONS

God used the half brother of Jesus to inscribe some unvarnished truths and hard solutions to the strain and injury our envy causes. This biblical passage perfectly lays out the experience of envy without ever mentioning the word by asking some thought-provoking questions, which we must take time to answer honestly. James begins by asking, "What causes quarrels and what causes fights among you?" (James 4:1a). In light of what I just explained, don't just pop off with Flip Wilson's retort, "The devil made me do it!"[18] Consider the strategy he is employing in your heart. James rushes right to the familiar diagnosis. "Is it not this, that your passions are at war within you?" (v. 1b). We know that we need to seek remedy for these transgressive unseen roots, but there they are, driving the relational breakdowns in our lives. I know the passions he is referring to clearly relate to envy because of the next two lines, "You desire and do not have, so you murder. You covet and cannot obtain, so you fight and quarrel" (v. 2). And what do we desire and covet? If it results in "murder" and "quarreling," it must be more than simply chasing after the similar things my friends possess—it must by definition involve full-grown hostility and bitterness toward them for having what I want. Whether it's their brains, brawn, or business acumen, we want what they have, and we don't like them for having it. James uses the word *murder*, and though no literal homicides were taking place in their Bible studies, the verbal assassinations of gossip and backstabbing were clearly out of control.

Perhaps the reason James uses the word *covet* instead of *envy* in verse 2 is because he is going to point out the selfish illusion of chasing after the things that other people in our lives possess. This coveting is the foundation for the envy, and it is nothing more than "wrongly asking" God for these things simply to "spend it on your passions" (v. 3). It's getting caught up in the false fantasy that having all the temporal blessings that the Joneses possess will make us happy and finally bring contentment. God used Solomon to give us this timeless wisdom: "He who loves money will not be satisfied with money, nor he who loves wealth with his income; this also is vanity" (Eccl. 5:10). The foolish passions at war within us are the problem. And they must be overcome.

I say the solution is hard because the passage couldn't be more dramatic in spelling out the initial phase of seeing the problem rectified. We can't recite a simple prayer or follow a set of easy steps. We must start with a full-blown hatred of our old ways, and the old values that still crop up in our Christian lives. It's a jarring call to take the problem seriously. It's another level deeper than what James wrote in the previous chapter about the "bitter jealousy and selfish ambition" that was damaging relationships being "earthly, unspiritual, demonic" (James 3:14–15). This is where he drops the serious indictment, and also where he introduces the solution. Read this passage slowly, humbly, and reflectively—carefully consider the topic of the sin of envy and the relational damage it causes. Note that it starts with admitting the worldly values that should be a thing of the past for us. Reflect on how pride, Satan, and the proper response to God's jealousy are all interlaced in this important text.

> You adulterous people! Do you not know that friendship with
> the world is enmity with God? Therefore whoever wishes
> to be a friend of the world makes himself an enemy of God.
> Or do you suppose it is to no purpose that the Scripture
> says, "He yearns jealously over the spirit that he has made to
> dwell in us"? But he gives more grace. Therefore it says, "God
> opposes the proud but gives grace to the humble." Submit
> yourselves therefore to God. Resist the devil, and he will flee
> from you. Draw near to God, and he will draw near to you.
> Cleanse your hands, you sinners, and purify your hearts, you
> double-minded. Be wretched and mourn and weep. Let your
> laughter be turned to mourning and your joy to gloom. Hum-
> ble yourselves before the Lord, and he will exalt you.
>    Do not speak evil against one another, brothers.
> (James 4:4–11a)

I want to unpack the heart of what it means to "draw near to God" as a very specific and practical remedy to envy, but first let's take a sobering look at some of the broadest damage this vice can cause—when it takes root in society at large.

## four

# THE SOCIETAL COSTS OF ENVY

**My older brother moved** to Kansas to pastor a church. Obviously, that state has a lot more inclement weather than where we grew up. Their weather forecasts mean a lot more to them—more than just deciding whether they should grab their umbrellas on the way out the door. In Tornado Alley, if there is a critical forecast for the upcoming afternoon, the weatherman will get on the TV and on social media and speak in foreboding terms like: "Warning! Severe Weather Alert! Conditions are developing for possible EF3 and EF4 tornadic activity!" It's all so dramatic.

I could head out to Kansas and change all of that. I could make an appointment to interview at the local television news station—promising the management that I will only bring good forecasts. I could tell them that I see all the trepidation and frustration those old fear-mongering forecasts are causing everybody in town, and I'm here to put an end to it. I will make everyone feel good again by promising to only forecast pleasant weather, in the most pleasant terms, no matter what!

Sweet idea from a nice guy. But a guy who is thoroughly disconnected from reality. And because of that, I'm pretty sure I wouldn't get the job. I can envision the boss saying, "Our forecasts are not broadcast to scare people, they are broadcast to prepare people!"

## GOD'S FORECAST

In His Word the Lord revealed that the present age will be punctuated by "wars and rumors of wars . . . nation will rise against nation, and kingdom against kingdom" (Matt. 24:6–7). And sadly, the Bible tells us we need to understand that all the conflicts, distrust, slander, and brutal activity will only ramp up "in the last days" (2 Tim. 3:1–5). At some point the brutality will be so universal that it will look a lot like it did in the days of Noah when God "saw that the wickedness of man was great in the earth, and that every intention of the thoughts of his heart was only evil continually" (Gen. 6:5). That is when the big storm of Christ's return and His associated judgments will begin to unfold (Rev. 6–19).

Throughout history we have already seen the rise and fall of kingdoms, empires, and world powers, which demonstrated the runaway debauchery, conflict, and implosion that will one day happen on the world stage. Once powerful and influential empires have fallen when the restraining hand of God has given them over to their insatiable appetite to do whatever they wanted. Consider this biblical description of a society that sounds all too familiar:

And since they did not see fit to acknowledge God, God gave them up to a debased mind to do what ought not to be done. They were filled with all manner of unrighteousness, evil, covetousness, malice. They are full of envy, murder, strife, deceit, maliciousness. They are gossips, slanderers, haters of God, insolent, haughty, boastful, inventors of evil, disobedient to parents, foolish, faithless, heartless, ruthless. Though they know God's righteous decree that those who practice such things deserve to die, they not only do them but give approval to those who practice them. (Rom. 1:28–32)

Notice what takes priority on the list, depicted as brimming over in the individual hearts of the citizens of this corrupted and strife-ridden society. Envy! They are "full of envy." And as we have seen, if that's what their hearts are full of, the next thing on the list follows—they are full of murder! They are filled with strife, deceit, maliciousness, gossip, slander, and the rest. In this kind of culture these traits are so normalized that the people are not ashamed of such things; they are not struck with guilt. Instead, they celebrate it all and pat each other on the back for doing such things. We can imagine this society applauding a specific sort of hero, loving a particular kind of music, enjoying a certain flavor of entertainment. We can envision their bestselling books, and the social media rants that the masses in such a culture would cheer on.

Throughout history, in moments of sobriety, when Christians reflect on their warring cultural swamp, they see it all clearly. Consider the words found inscribed on the inside of a German Bible dating back to the seventeenth century—during the time of Europe's Thirty Years' War: "Everywhere there is envy, hatred and greed: that's what the war has taught us. . . . We live like animals."[19]

Few sins damage a society more than insidious, unfettered envy in the hearts of men, women, and children. That's not a warning meant to scare, but a truth designed to prepare us for the society in which we now live.

## ENVIOUS CULTURAL CONFLICT

The headlines depicting the strife in our society are an ongoing cautionary tale of the havoc envy would wreak in our souls and in our churches if this deadly sin were not identified and combated in our lives. It doesn't take much reflection to realize that the root of so much of the anger, frustration, and hostility in our society is fueled by the discontent and resentment of envy. Riots and revolutions have been stirred up by a long line of infamous agitators who have highlighted the disparities between one group and another, shouting at their generation to rise up and join the fight to demand more, and to obliterate the societal imbalances.

Just as the church can degenerate into sparring groups that shout, "I'm of Paul" and "I'm of Apollos," there is an unbridled segment of our culture that hurls its warring chants of "I'm of us" and "You're of them!" Listen carefully beneath the sound bites and video clips and you will inevitably hear the familiar refrain of "I cannot stand them for having what I do not have!" If this were covetousness or simply greed, one would find people sad, depressed, or defeated. But as it is—they are angry, hostile, and vindictive. Our society is rife with conflict, violence, and enmity because it is brimming over with envy.

As one economist recently reminded a room full of stockholders,

The world is not driven by greed. It's driven by envy. And so the fact that everybody's five times better off than they used to be, they take it for granted. All they think about is somebody else has more now, and it's not fair that he should have it and they don't.[20]

Looking askance at those who have what I don't—even if I've got plenty to eat, a comfortable place to sleep, healthcare, medicines, a smartphone, and access to the internet—is always a temptation. We look up the row at those financially better off and say, "I *need* what they have" and it most certainly "isn't fair" that they get to enjoy what I don't. This is the foundational discontent that gives birth to the anger and hostility toward the "haves" which necessarily follows.

## THE DESTRUCTIVE POWER OF ENVY

When reading the Bible, it doesn't take long to come across frenzied groups of people teaming together against their perceived societal rivals out of envious resentment. And the consequences are always destructive. It is Cain and Abel all over again, but on a much larger scale.

I suppose one could argue that there was an envious undertone in Genesis 11, when the budding population at Babel rushed to measure up to heaven itself. As they crafted their tower to the heavens, we can imagine the architects saying, "There will be no second-rate assessment of us." Of course, their self-aggrandizing project ended in a humbling confusion and dispersion.

During the wilderness wanderings of Israel, after the mass exodus from Egypt, a faction of grumbling malcontents envied the privileges of Moses and his leadership team, and decided that enough was enough; we are all important and should all have equal power in this nation (Num. 16:3). They accused Moses of "exalting himself," when in fact it was God who had blessed and appointed Moses to his leadership post—along with all of its associated pressures and problems. God, as some might remember, opened up the ground and swallowed hundreds of these rebels, bringing them to an immediate death, and providing a memorable example to keep our envious hostilities in check.

In the days of Samuel the prophet, the people of Israel enviously fixated on keeping up appearances with the other nations. They wanted a human king and felt that they were disadvantaged if they didn't have one (1 Sam. 8:19–20; 12:10–12). God had clearly been providing all that the nation needed. For hundreds of years, when they faced a military threat, God was gracious to raise up the right provisional leader who would assemble an army to defeat Israel's foes. The track record was impressive. God was providing. But they saw a power inequity, even when it really proved to be no material threat. So the people clamored, moaned, complained, and whined, and God, as He often does, turned them over to their sinful hearts, which at the time were burning with envy. After warning them, He gave them what they wanted and told Samuel that they hadn't rejected the prophet, they had in fact rejected God, and would soon incur a variety of costly repercussions (1 Sam. 8:7).

The Bible provides us with many historical circumstances where envious cravings and hostile efforts to ensure that no one gets any special treatment, exceptional access, or unique privileges all backfire, and God has to say with painful emphasis, "I'll do with my creatures what I please." And that He certainly does.

## GOD'S VARIED BLESSINGS AND TRIALS

Let me ask you: Why didn't you give any TED Talks last month? Why aren't you lecturing at Cambridge and Oxford this fall? Why didn't you sign a multimillion-dollar contract for an NBA team last year? Why haven't you been posing for more fashion magazine covers lately? And why have you yet to win an Emmy, Grammy, Oscar, and Tony Award all in the same year?

Well, I know why I haven't. No one's asking me. And for good reason—I'm not designed nor gifted to do any of those things.

And I need to be okay with that. Thankfully, right now I am. And I should be. At least my mom never told me I could do anything I wanted or could be anyone I wanted to be. Whew. Thanks, Mom! She kindly didn't set me up for disappointment and gratefully didn't feed my naturally inclined envious heart.[21]

Speaking of parenting for just a minute, back in chapter 2 I briefly quoted William Law, the Cambridge grad who preached back at the turn of the eighteenth century. He had a lot to say about the way parents can feed the sinful inclination to envy in their children. In educating their kids, most parents fail to help them appreciate the varied grace of God, which He demonstrates by sovereignly dispensing very *unequal* gifts, talents, and blessings. Here's a brief portion of William's concern—it contains some antiquated language but it's definitely worth the read.

> You teach a child to scorn to be outdone, to thirst for distinction and applause; and is it any wonder that he continues to act all his life in the same manner?
>
> Now if a youth is ever to be so far a Christian, as to govern his heart by the doctrines of humility, I would fain know at what time he is to begin it: or, if he is ever to begin it at all, why we train him up in tempers quite contrary to it?
>
> How dry and poor must the doctrine of humility sound to a youth, that has been spurred up to all his industry by ambition, envy, emulation, and a desire of glory and distinction? And if he is not to act by these principles when he is a man, why do we call him to act by them in his youth?
>
> Envy is acknowledged by all people, to be the most ungenerous, base and wicked passion, that can enter into the heart of man.
>
> And is this a temper to be instilled, nourished and established, in the minds of young people?

I know it is said, that it is not envy, but emulation, that is intended to be awakened in the minds of young men.

But this is vainly said. For when children are taught to bear no rival, and to scorn to be out-done by any of their age, they are plainly and directly taught to be envious. For it is impossible for any one to have this scorn of being out-done, and this contention with rivals, without burning with envy against all those that seem to excel him, or get any distinction from him. So that what children are taught, is rank envy, and only covered with a name of a less odious sound.[22]

When I talk about rejoicing in *your lot in life*—i.e., "contentment" (Eccl. 3:22)—I always need to state that I don't mean to disallow, or in any way discourage, the diligent *selfless* ambition of being a great steward of the gifts God has entrusted to you! You're likely not in the NBA. Okay. Fine. Well, what is it then that God has gifted you to do and set you here to accomplish? As God's Word says, "Whatever you do, work heartily" (Col. 3:23a), which is not a cover for the "emulation" William Law talked about (that word doesn't mean to mimic; in his context it means striving to outdo everyone else in your class, field, or career). As the next part of that verse in Colossians states, our work is supposed to be done "as for the Lord, and not for men." It's not ultimately for people, or with a competitive view of people, or to impress people, or to measure myself by the work of people. It is about recognizing God's sovereign equipping in my own life and living humbly, lovingly, and productively in the field where God has planted me.

## SOVEREIGN VARIETY

God's sovereignty. This is one of the toughest doctrines in the Bible. Not for the reason you might think, but simply because it comes down to this—God is God and you're not. Really, that's it. Forget for now all the conundrums, seeming paradoxes, and mind-bending antinomies. The toughest part of this doctrine is that you didn't make any of the decisions about where you were born, when you were born, to whom you were born, how tall you would be, what color your eyes would be, how your entire genetic code would be programmed, etc., etc. I could go on, but you would be tempted to object. That's what all rational created beings tend to do. They are tempted to object to God being God. We'd like that role, at least in our own lives, thank you very much! Let me call the shots. Let me think I get to determine and decree everything. We'd like to think like that, but at least at the outset of my list I trust you felt powerless—as though you were not God. When you don't feel like God, that's a good thing.

When Paul was lecturing the professors of Athens in Acts 17, he began with some fundamental truths that were supposed to help get his audience on the right footing.

> "The God who made the world and everything in it, being Lord of heaven and earth, does not live in temples made by man, nor is he served by human hands, as though he needed anything, since he himself gives to all mankind life and breath and everything. And he made from one man every nation of mankind to live on all the face of the earth, having determined allotted periods and the boundaries of their dwelling place." (Acts 17:24–26)

Paul reminds us that there is a God, and we are not Him. He has not only determined where and when you exist, but He is actively giving you life right now.

That is helpful. Particularly for our topic. The more I can process this reality, the less I will foolishly pine away that I'm not Jim,

Tom, or Ryan. Not only do I not have the gifts, skills, or talents of those guys, but I also can't fly, I can't be born in the fifth century, I can't live in the center of the earth, and I can't be a turnip. I need to learn the basic reality that has been echoed in one way or another by God throughout His Book:

> Shall the ax boast over him who hews with it, or the saw magnify itself against him who wields it? As if a rod should wield him who lifts it, or as if a staff should lift him who is not wood! (Isa. 10:15)

> But who are you, O man, to answer back to God? Will what is molded say to its molder, "Why have you made me like this?" Has the potter no right over the clay, to make out of the same lump one vessel for honorable use and another for dishonorable use? (Rom. 9:20–21)

And when it comes to gifts or blessings in my life and yours, the Bible has been trying to drill into our minds, "each has his own gift from God, one of one kind and one of another" (1 Cor. 7:7). The great news is that if you are reading this, you have been granted life, and are created by God in His image to glorify Him. As a Christian, how great it is to look past the things I don't have and affirm with God's Word that "there are varieties of gifts, but the same Spirit; and there are varieties of service, but the same Lord; and there are varieties of activities, but it is the same God who empowers them all in everyone" (1 Cor. 12:4–6). That is dignifying, encouraging, and motivating. God made me, gifted me, equipped me, and will work through me. I'm not you, and you're not me. So let's stop comparing and resenting each other for what I enjoy and you don't, and what you enjoy and I don't.

That might be all fine and good to you at this point, but I know there's an objection coming. You may say, "Wait a minute, that's all great if I'm a running back and you're a middle linebacker— even on days that I'd rather be the middle linebacker! But I'm not even on the field! I feel like I'm consigned to be the vendor selling hotdogs in the nosebleed seats!" Well, I get that. You make a good point. It's one thing to be tempted to be the quarterback when I'm the wide receiver. But what if I'm on the stadium maintenance crew, and I want to be the quarterback? Perhaps I could take solace in the fact that I'm catching passes instead of throwing them. "But come on man, I'm unclogging the restroom toilets!"

Are you following all of that? It's like the mom who is tempted to envy the other mom because her daughter got the lead role in the play, and her daughter is in some supporting role. But what about the woman who longs to be a mom? How is the single woman who can't even get a date supposed to muscle up and not get envious of the mom whose daughter got the lead in the play? The "gap" seems too great. Where is the hope? Where can I find comfort in a God who has, in His sovereignty, apparently consigned me to a life without children or even a husband?

There are answers. There is hope. There is sustaining grace, favor, and strength from God that makes the consistent defeat of envy and a contented life possible. But it will always come back to God's sovereignty.

My daughter was born with a congenital birth defect that has required multiple surgeries and has left her paralyzed from the knees down. She does not have what you might call a normal life. But it is her "normal." You can imagine how that kind of diagnosis makes you lean into a kind of parenting that understands more of the realities of a sovereign set of decisions from God, and keeps you from saying, "Hey, honey, you can be whatever you want to be and do whatever you want to do!" Well, that sentence isn't true for her, nor for you. But if you have a child like mine, it certainly keeps you from saying silly things as often. If she was your daughter and exclaimed one morning, "I want to play soccer," or "I want to be a dancer," or "I want to get up and run down the sidewalk," you would need to provide her with uncommon responses that function within the sovereign choices of God.

Before you think, *Oh, how sad*, please don't. We know that not being able to walk is a disability—we don't play mind games in my home or try to ignore reality! My daughter doesn't want you to be consumed with pity or sadness about her condition. When you meet her, she doesn't need any of that, though she might need your help with something else. And her goal is not to be consumed with envy. She understands there is plenty in your life that limits you, just as there is in hers. And she also knows there are plenty of things you might truly want that other people have and enjoy. We all have our divinely and sovereignly chosen trials. I wrote an entire book on my daughter's trials and this topic to help us think about ours.[23] However, we can all say, as Paul said concerning his trial (when he asked God to remove it and God didn't), that no matter what the deprivation, God's grace is sufficient for us because His power is made perfect in weakness (2 Cor. 12:9).

## HUMILITY AND THANKSGIVING

We certainly can't singlehandedly change the society in which we live. It brims with envy filling the hearts of competitive and resentful people. And the forecast doesn't show it letting up. Instead, our goal is to worship and give thanks. Such noble and godly actions take into consideration the realities that most in this world currently refuse to acknowledge. There is a God, and He is kind enough to give us life and breath and whatever else it is that we have. Being grateful in all circumstances is the safeguard against us getting caught up in what the world is clawing after and stabbing each other in the back to get. We have a gracious and powerful Father who has provided this planet with a tremendously varied group of people.

While we will want many things in this life—sincerely and rightly want—some of them God will give to us, while others He surely won't. There will be pains we want God to relieve, and in some cases He may bring the relief, but in other cases we can be sure He will not. But either way, we will purpose to be the counter-cultural ones in this generation who realize that the ultimate gifts, along with the fulfillment that will truly and finally satisfy, lay beyond this life. We need to see that even when temporal gifts are given, like they were to Hannah in the Old Testament, and even when the gift is something as precious as a child—the true and lasting gift, even in this life, is knowing our God.

As Jeremiah said, the thing to treasure is not treasures. The wise man shouldn't treasure his wisdom, nor the strong man his strength, nor the rich man his riches. The Oxford professors should not treasure their scholarly achievements and the NBA players should not treasure their stats or contracts. Jeremiah reminds us that the thing to treasure and the reality to boast in (if it happens to be true of you) is that you understand and know the Lord (Jer. 9:23–24). Nothing else really matters. Which brings me back to Hannah.

Hannah, if you remember, was infertile and like many in her situation truly wanted a child. She prayed fervently and was tempted to envy the women who were swaddling their babies and teaching their kids to walk. But surprisingly, when God gave her the very thing she asked for, do you remember what she did with that little baby named Samuel? She so treasured the God who sovereignly granted her that baby that she "gave him back" to the Lord. She dropped him off at the worship center and traveled back to her home. Unthinkable for most of us! How could you value the Giver more than the gift, when the gift was your little baby son? She could and she did. I know she did because of her words recorded in the next chapter—words we can learn from as we seek to contentedly affirm the realities the world knows nothing about. Hannah prayed,

"There is none holy like the LORD:
    for there is none besides you;
    there is no rock like our God.
Talk no more so very proudly,
    let not arrogance come from your mouth;
for the LORD is a God of knowledge,
    and by him actions are weighed.
The bows of the mighty are broken,
    but the feeble bind on strength.
Those who were full have hired themselves out for bread,
    but those who were hungry have ceased to hunger.
The barren has borne seven,
    but she who has many children is forlorn.
The LORD kills and brings to life;
    he brings down to Sheol and raises up.
The LORD makes poor and makes rich;
    he brings low and he exalts.
He raises up the poor from the dust;
    he lifts the needy from the ash heap
to make them sit with princes
    and inherit a seat of honor." (1 Sam. 2:2–8)

# COUNTERATTACK ON ENVY: EVALUATE

**He was in his prime** a hundred years ago. He was the heavyweight boxing champion of the world. His name was Jack Dempsey, and he was a revered and feared social celebrity in the 1920s. A big, strong, forceful champ who often summarized his tactical strategy in a single sentence. This line was picked up by the culture and you've probably even said it yourself. His famous line? "The best defense is a good offense!"[24]

The hundreds of times that Dempsey stepped into the ring, he wasn't just trying to keep himself from being hit or knocked out; his focus was on attacking his opponent and landing blows that would neutralize the threat. His international fame made his hometown of Manassa, Colorado, proud. His approach to fighting earned him the name Manassa Mauler, along with a professional record of sixty-eight wins—fifty-three of them by knockout.

We have been working to identify a formidable foe in the Christian life, one that has infected relationships, churches, workplaces, and even our culture at large. It has piled up a heap of victims along the way, ending friendships, splitting congregations, destroying all sorts of relationships, not to mention creating loads of discontent, suspicion, and resentment in the hearts of those overtaken by it.

Our job in the next three chapters is to look at the biblical defense. But better than ducking our heads and hoping that we can survive the onslaught of envy's temptations coming at us from every side, we will affirm that Dempsey was on the right track, and seek to launch the best defense of all—a biblical counterattack. We have to be aggressive to defeat this opponent of our godliness, joy, and contentment. And it starts with knowing where to hit. But first, we have to return to the root of envy and make some important distinctions—that way we can know exactly when we are being attacked.

## BEWARE OF THE LEAVEN

Even Pontius Pilate could see that the Pharisees were envious of Jesus. And reminiscent of Cain's homicide in Genesis 4, these Jewish leaders were now engaged with the Romans in a conspiracy to commit murder. Their resentment of Christ and His growing fame had descended into a kind of hatred that allowed the "religious" teachers to justify their part in killing the one they detested. Why? Because this itinerant rabbi from Nazareth was stealing their spotlight.

Jesus could easily see the selfish longings of the Pharisees and Sadducees. He saw their self-promotion and the runaway pride that led them to want to grab the spotlight in any situation they could. They craved the attention and adulation of the crowds, and this was made obvious by where they strategized to sit at banquets, how they dressed themselves, and even in how they worded and articulated their public prayers (Mark 12:39; Matt. 6:5; 23:5). With all this self-interest contaminating the instruction of the nation's leaders, Jesus told His followers to "watch and beware of the leaven of the Pharisees and Sadducees" (Matt. 16:6).

Jesus knew that their strong self-centered desires would be the foundation for all sorts of sins—even the insidious malevolence of envy that would motivate the conspiracy to have Him executed (Matt. 27:18). This "leaven," if left unchecked, will inevitably creep into every aspect of a person's motives and grow into the rivalries and hostilities that are rightly defined as envy.

Never having baked bread, I've only heard all the secondhand chatter from those who do. They talk of yeast and the beloved starters for their sourdough loaves. It is fascinating to hear of the seemingly tireless power and enduring processes of these tiny additions of specialized bacteria and fungi that just keep doing their thing to make possible an endless amount of tasty bread. That's enough information for me to know why leaven is a perfect illustration for how such a small thing has a seemingly endless intrinsic power to affect the whole of my life, my church, and my society.

It is also interesting that in the book of Exodus, when God institutes Israel's annual commemoration of His deliverance of the people from Egyptian enslavement, He wanted them to go a full week every year without any leaven in their homes. Everything had to be made without the use of yeast. But more than that, they had to eradicate it from every corner of their cupboards, kitchens, and homes (Ex. 12:14–20). No leaven. Anywhere! While the absence of leaven in their bread was a reminder that they scurried out of Egypt quickly (vv. 33–34), the symbolism ran much deeper. They were to leave more than the leaven behind. They were to be "holy"—different, unique, morally unlike the society they left. They were to be without a lot of the things that surrounded and often infected their former lives. And so it was that Jesus pointed out how easily a little of those sinful values will overtake the motives of a person's life if given a chance.

In Titus 3:3, God uses Paul to remind us that we have to extract many of the things that characterized our pre-Christian days: "we ourselves were once foolish, disobedient, led astray, slaves to various passions and pleasures, passing our days in malice and envy, hated by others and hating one another." The daily battle in the Christian life begins by identifying the problem.

## DO NOT COVET WHAT?

Eight chapters after God initiates the weeklong call to extract all the leaven, He gives Israel a set of fundamental rules that, when followed, would truly characterize them as unique. They would be a holy and distinct people as they sought to arrange their society and their moral lives around the ten central commands, which were to characterize this fledgling nation. Of course, we know them as the Ten Commandments, and they end with a prohibition that has much to do with the problem of envy. As a matter of fact, you can't have envy without first being embroiled in the violation of the tenth commandment. It begins with, "You shall not covet . . ." (Ex. 20:17a).

Unlike many of the other commands on that list, which simply consist of "don't do this, don't do that," the tenth one continues on. Several of the preceding prohibitions are very brief. "You shall not murder," "You shall not commit adultery," "You shall not steal"

(vv. 13–15). Those are all short and to the point. Why did the tenth command not just end there? Because it really couldn't. At least not without being really confusing to the original recipients.

In the Hebrew language of the Old Testament, the word translated as "covet" in Exodus 20:17 (an English verb employed in our Bibles to consistently represent a sinful vice) is often used as a good and appropriate action. The word *hamad* is first introduced in Genesis 2:9 as a good thing. It is translated into English as the adjective "pleasant," because the context is a good one. It is found as a description of the varieties of fruit trees in the garden of Eden which are "pleasant" or "desirable" (and perfectly allowable) to provide food for Adam and Eve. The word describes what you might think and feel if you were hungry and walked into the family dining room on Thanksgiving and saw a beautiful spread of appetizing foods on the table. And assuming that you were not crashing someone else's party, even the most pious among us would enjoy that thought and feeling without any hint of guilt or shame. That desire is a good thing, and God intended for us to find satisfaction and enjoyment in having that experience (1 Tim. 4:3–4).

I use the Thanksgiving table example in hopes of getting you to see that this Hebrew word *hamad* is more than just having a plain old desire or run-of-the-mill appetite for something. The idea here is to *really want* something, to even *crave* that something. Even so, this word depicting strong desire is used in a positive sense in about half of the twenty-one times it is employed in the Hebrew Old Testament. Consider also the New Testament Greek word *epithumia*, which often translates into the word *lust*, and when it does it usually carries a negative connotation, as in the call to control our sexual cravings and be holy, "not in the passion of lust like the Gentiles who do not know God" (1 Thess. 4:5). And yet, it might surprise you, this same Greek word *epithumia* is employed in a commendable sense, when Paul writes to Timothy about prospective pastors in Ephesus and says, "If anyone aspires to the office of overseer, he [*epithumias*] a noble task" (1 Tim. 3:1). Here the translations don't use the English word *lust*, but use the word *desire*. So these similar words in both Testaments imply a strong inclination, attraction, or craving, but they can refer to something good and righteous as well as to something bad and sinful.

Since the Hebrew word *hamad* is often used in the Old Testament in a good and appropriate sense, you can understand why God could not make the tenth commandment in Exodus 20 as short as the others. "You shall not *hamad*" would be confusing. It would be akin to hearing in English: "You shall not strongly desire." I suppose you could try to be a potted plant for the rest of your life, and pretend you're not really hungry when you are, or that you really don't want to tackle some noble project when you do, but in reality there would be no way to square that with the rest of the Bible. So, God clarifies and removes the possibility of confusion for those Hebrew speakers by elaborating:

> "You shall not covet your neighbor's house; you shall not covet your neighbor's wife, or his male servant, or his female servant, or his ox, or his donkey, or anything that is your neighbor's." (Ex. 20:17)

Do you see the emphasis? Do you catch the qualification? The strong desire is not the problem, it's the strong desire for things that someone else already rightly possesses. Those are their relationships, their resources, their riches. They belong to someone else, and your longing and strong desire is to have what is already in their possession.

You might think, "Well then, this sounds like a concern about the seeds of motivation for someone engaging in theft or adultery."

Sure, that is certainly true. But I think even here in this context, it is a prohibition that is segmented out from the others because these runaway daydreams and desires serve as the doorway to envy's spiraling melancholy, which ruminates on the fact that we don't get to have what *they* have, along with the festering annoyance at our neighbors, friends, and brothers for all their surpassing advantages and blessings.

## THE WORLD'S DEFAULT CRAVINGS

When it comes to strong desires, the envious non-Christian world is not only unabashed in bragging that they have them—plenty of them, but they are experts in stoking them and indiscriminately unleashing them. Indiscriminate—that's the problem. The seemingly aimless, haphazard, all-over-the-place quest for satisfaction is the biblical problem. It is what makes quenching those strong desires a transgressive problem.

I mentioned that the first use of the Hebrew word *hamad* is God's description of the desirable trees that He had put in the garden for His newly created couple to enjoy. He knew they would be hungry. Sometimes really hungry. From time to time famished. Well, God had an appropriate solution: trees that were desirable and appropriate to consume and satisfy their appetites. But, as you know, Eve had a wandering eye and a serious temptation to go after another tree in the garden—the one that was off limits. God had said of that one tree, "You shall not eat [of it]" (Gen. 2:17). Isn't it interesting that the second employment of the Hebrew word *hamad* was descriptive of Eve's heart amid her temptation? It says she had been lured by the beauty of that fruit and the lies of the tempter to feel that this off-limits tree was "[*hamad*] to make one wise" (Gen. 3:6). It was a "covetable" tree! It stirred up strong

desires. Adam and Eve's challenge of living in the garden with al-
luring trees was making the right distinctions between appropriate
targets for their strong desires as opposed to inappropriate ones.

Ever since, the world has worked to enshrine Eve's indiscriminate quest for satisfaction as every person's fundamental right.
All around us the culture preaches that whatever random strong
desire you have, it's sacrosanct. And how those strong desires are
quenched hardly needs to be debated. "If it feels good, do it," they
say. The value has become: "The supremely important thing is
your unfettered freedom to pursue what you want, wherever, and
whenever you want it."

The New Testament speaks to the folly of this error:

Do not love the world or the things in the world. If anyone
loves the world, the love of the Father is not in him. For all
that is in the world—the desires of the flesh and the desires
of the eyes and pride of life—is not from the Father but is
from the world. And the world is passing away along with
its desires, but whoever does the will of God abides forever.
(1 John 2:15–17)

Much like the Old Testament command to not covet, we must
carefully define and understand what is and isn't being said here.
If you exhorted me: "Don't love anything in the world!" and I say,
"But my mother is in the world, and my wife is in the world, and
my church is in the world, and my Bible is in the world!," you
might say, "Well, I didn't mean *those* things." And you shouldn't,
because God has indeed told us to love plenty that is in the world.
This first line is clearly qualified in context by the explanation between the dashes. The kind of love the world demonstrates, their
commitments, loyalties, and priorities, and the quests they pursue

are all wrong when they do so based on the criteria of the indiscriminate—the desires of the flesh, the desires of the eyes, and the pride of life.

Human flesh has a lot of desires. Some are appropriate and some are out of bounds. First, there is a kind of love, passion, and appetite that says, *Whatever my flesh desires I'm going to get it.* Again, it's the indiscriminate, haphazard, and unrestrained quest for whatever fleshly impulses strongly surface—these are clearly out of bounds. Second, our eyes are attracted to a lot of things, just like Eve's. But whatever sparkles and lures our eyes, thoughts, and imaginations isn't necessarily appropriate. It's the unbridled mindset of "If it really looks good to you, get it!" Third, and in a sense foundationally, the pride of life; this shows us why we don't care about whether the thing we want belongs to our neighbor or not—because it is for *me* and is all about *me*! Eve was willing to go after an off-limit craving because it looked good to *her*, she thought it would be satisfying to *her*, and she was convinced it would make *her* wise. The self-concerned, self-satisfying, self-exalting interest of Eve is much like the interest of the world in which we live. The real hazard is that the quest of our current society is to lay out as many options as possible, so that we are able to pursue whatever fleshly impulse, attractive focus, or self-satisfying thing we want. Forget the boundaries; there are no confines, fences, or prohibitions in the amusement park of modern culture.

## POLICE YOUR CRAVINGS

My dad was a cop in Long Beach. As a kid, when he was in uniform, he looked to me like I would expect Jack Dempsey to look if he were wearing police blue. My dad was an imposing figure of strength and enforcement—twirling his baton as he patrolled on foot to keep the peace in the downtown district. Much of his job, like most police officers, was not employing those tools of enforcement but walking his beat, looking around, being seen, and reminding the people frequenting those businesses that he could at any moment actively make use of his tools and engage in the work of enforcement. That's a bit of how I'd like you to feel as you patrol through the avenues of your heart and mind and begin to "look around" at what's going on in there.

It is my prayer that God will empower you—even now as you take in these words—to be as objective as possible, and with the help of God's Spirit to start to sort through everything in your inner life that qualifies as a strong desire. I want you to do so soberly, as though you are carrying high caliber tools for implementing some serious enforcement. After all, when it comes to what you may discover, this is where it might lead. Here are some previews:

> Put to death therefore what is earthly in you: sexual immorality, impurity, passion, evil desire, and covetousness. (Col. 3:5)

> But I discipline my body and keep it under control, lest after preaching to others I myself should be disqualified. (1 Cor. 9:27)

> For just as you once presented your members as slaves to impurity and to lawlessness leading to more lawlessness, so now present your members as slaves to righteousness leading to sanctification. (Rom. 6:19b)

Okay, with that in mind, and knowing that you may need to do some painful spiritual work on what you find, take a slow and honest stroll through your heart—opening every door, pulling back every curtain, and shining a bright flashlight into every corner.

What you are looking for is anything that you would say is something "you really want," anything "you truly desire," something you have to admit is a "craving." Conduct an exhaustive investigation until you've taken stock of all the things you know your thoughts come back to again and again. Itemize the things you find yourself fondly daydreaming about. Take stock of every person, place, or thing that accelerates your pulse and raises your eyebrows with a piqued interest.

Now let's put those desires into two boxes: "Quash" or "Keep." This is where you have to be careful not to let the subliminal rationalizations that so often accompany our covetousness to surface and affect your present evaluation. Go through each recurring desire and ask the following:

1. Is this particular and specific object or experience in any way prohibited by God's Word?

2. Is this desired thing or person something I have a legitimate godly right to have?

3. Would the fulfillment of this craving be in some way about self-promotion, personal adulation, or selfish, self-serving ambition?

I could go on, but this quick set of questions, which summarizes the wise instructions throughout the Bible, is usually enough for me to place my cravings into one box or the other. Now you know what to do. Time to severely quash the contents of the "Quash" box. Read the rule in Colossians 3:5 again. (Here, I'll help: "Put them to death!") Starve them. Choke them. Attack them. Assault them. Declare war on them, because if you don't, you'll be left resembling the New Testament false teachers who make it their habit to aid and abet whatever indiscriminate desires they find within. The unvarnished truth is that these kinds of decisions reveal that "such persons do not serve our Lord Christ, but their own appetites" (Rom. 16:18). That may seem harsh, but hold your hat, the Bible goes on: "Their end is destruction, their god is their belly, and they glory in their shame, with minds set on earthly things" (Phil. 3:19).

Sorting through our desires and deciding to "Dempsey" our transgressive passions will sometimes feel like the frustrating game of Whac-A-Mole. I assume you've played it. As soon as you think you've scored a point and defeated the culprit, the mole or one of his cousins pops up on the other side of the grid. Your heart has lots of recesses. Your strong illicit desires can pop up here and then at a different time over there. So you'll have to stay nimble and vigilant; the work of identifying and understanding what's going on in your desires is an ongoing task. Just as my dad couldn't walk his downtown beat once and call it a day, you're going to have to go back to the same places and keep shining the light into the crevasses of your soul.

## AIMED AND AMPLIFIED CRAVINGS

The good news is that you placed things into two boxes. I hope the "Keep" box wasn't empty. But if it wasn't as full as the "Quash" box, there is some good work to be done. Frankly, when you thoughtfully engage in this next step it will simultaneously serve to starve the covetous desires of your mind's focus and attention, as well as fill the "Keep" box.

Christians have a calling to crave things that have eternal consequence. First and foremost, the highest and strongest desire we should cultivate is to want to know the Eternal One. Paul testifies to how this ultimate longing inherently starts to move other desires to the periphery. "Indeed, I count everything as loss because of the surpassing worth of knowing Christ Jesus my Lord" (Phil. 3:8). There's a great phrase: "the surpassing worth." Here is something that when it is nurtured and favored in your daily priorities will necessarily start to push out lesser cravings. The author of Psalm 42, who was clearly a lap or two ahead of most of us, wrote about his strong craving with the following lyrics: "As a deer pants for flowing streams, so pants my soul for you, O God. My soul thirsts for God, for the living God" (Ps. 42:1–2). Guess what he had little internal bandwidth for? All the other cravings that were off limits!

When the worthiest desire makes the top of the list, and is rightly aimed and amplified, then Jeremiah 9:23–24 isn't a conviction in my life, it is the description of my life!

> "Let not the wise man boast in his wisdom, let not the mighty man boast in his might, let not the rich man boast in his riches, but let him who boasts boast in this, that he understands and knows me, that I am the LORD who practices steadfast love, justice, and righteousness in the earth. For in these things I delight, declares the LORD." (Jer. 9:23–24)

Not only do I not "boast in them," I don't chase after them and I don't resentfully envy those who have more wisdom, power, or riches than I do.

By the way, did you catch that last line? This is what God desires. This is what God delights in. And that's where you want to be. Right there—in the place God wants you to be. It's the kind of reality that could lead you to contentedly sing hymns of praise late into the night, even when you are sore from a beating and have been jailed and unjustly accused by a mob—or when you are facing whatever "woe-is-me" circumstances or setbacks that make you and your peers feel like life stinks (see Acts 16:22–25).

## GODLY AMBITIONS

The man or woman who craves to know and understand God does not only have one ambition. His or her heart is directed by a number of other godly passions. They are all related, but aimed at a number of goals and objectives.

When Paul, who sees all other desires as "nothing" compared to the value of knowing Christ, stepped into his work week, that supreme craving allowed him to sort out and set in place all the other desires of his life. Amid his busy schedule of tent-making, traveling, and preaching he declared, "I do not account my life of any value nor as precious to myself, if only I may finish my course and the ministry that I received from the Lord Jesus, to testify to the gospel of the grace of God" (Acts 20:24).

Notice he does not consider his life of any value nor as precious *to himself.* Not that you or I listening to him say that wouldn't blurt out, "Hey, Paul, your life is certainly of value and precious to us!" And that would be true; Paul also shared that perspective of so many of his friends (e.g., Phil. 2:25–30). But while he knew his life was incredibly beneficial to others, he had no interest in self-actualization! He wasn't about grabbing all the gusto in life that he could. No, he made tents with skill and integrity because he knew his life as a whole was going to serve to testify of Christ in this world. He traveled, but not for the same reason most people travel today—he didn't *live* to soak in all the beautiful sunsets on the Mediterranean (although I'm sure he enjoyed many). Paul's life was about finishing all the good in this world that God had designed him to fulfill. His godly ambition was to do what God had called him to do, and to be the missionary that God had called him to be.

Reading of Paul's life in the book of Acts, and getting a good picture of the man in his letters, we learn of a person who worked hard, strived for excellence, did his job better than most (if not all) of his contemporaries, but all for a very different motivation than most people. He saw his godly aspirations as Christ-serving, gospel-exalting, and God-honoring. He sought in every way to glorify his Maker.

## WANT WHAT YOU HAVE

That did not mean that God gave Paul everything he wanted. He clearly desired—strongly desired—many things that God did not grant him. There were health challenges, foiled missions, failed relationships, and closed doors to opportunities he really and rightly craved. Paul could have doggedly latched on to those good and godly things that he had determined were biblically allowable, righteously desired, and God-honoring. Just as you might latch on to the things in your "Keep" box.

The first step in our counterattack against envy was to weed out and turn our backs on the off-limits passions. But beyond that, we must come to recognize that our sovereign God may reach in and toss out some of the things that are legitimately okay for us to want. Ouch, that smarts! It hurts because we prayed for them, pursued them, and desired them. It might be as godly as getting married and having a child. It could be as reasonable as growing old with the wife of my youth. It can seem as good and prudent as purchasing a house and utilizing it for ministry. It might be as virtuous as desiring a seminary education and pursuing a ministry post in a church. I could go on, but you get the point.

Several of these sorts of desires you will have diligently pursued, but the door will be closed, and God will say "No more!" In reflecting on Paul's life it is helpful to see how agile he was—how quickly he would say, "Okay, then, I will do this or go there instead!" Even in that oft-quoted scene of his life when he "pleaded with the Lord" to take away his physical ailment (2 Cor. 12:8). What gets me every time is he says he pleaded *only* "three times." Wow. I've had plenty of painful problems in my body, and I have to say, I find it hard to believe that Paul only asked God three times.

Surely Paul knew Christ's instructions about persistent praying. Yet in times of disappointment, he changed his valuations of the things he desired. He decided to want what he had. He decided to align his secondary passions with the "yeses" and "nos" of God. While physical health may seem like something we would all rightly and tenaciously value and put near the top of our desires lists, Paul obviously did not. He knew how to take a "no" from God and realign his cravings. For the sake of the Person he craved the most, he chose to want what he was sovereignly given, knowing God's promised and enduring favor on his life was enough— and that if he wasn't dead yet, he hadn't finished the course. It didn't take him long to come to grips with the circumstances that showed him God was reaching into his "Keep" box of desires and saying, "We're not going to keep this."

Though Paul's desires for his daily life, relationships, and career were clearly connected to his supreme desire to know and love God, he was resolved to never make an idol out of a secondary passion. He knew, and we should too, that it is not only unrighteous desires that can prompt coveting and envy, but righteous ones as well. Our challenge, safeguard, and effective counterattack is to regularly do the hard work of assessing what's going on in our hearts.

six

# COUNTERATTACK ON ENVY: LOVE

**When Hagar was cradling** her infant son, Ishmael, in her arms, Sarah's eye went bad (as Jesus would say) and the squinty, cockeyed, dirty looks she gave the new mother revealed her festering envy. As Genesis 16:4–5 tells us, "She looked on her with contempt."

When Saul, the commander in chief of Israel's fighting forces, started to hear how the people sang the praises of the successful young warrior named David, his furrowed brow and piercing stare showed that envy had taken root in his heart: "Saul was very angry. . . . And Saul eyed David from that day on" (1 Sam. 18:8–9).

Having a child is a good thing. Being capable and successful in one's profession is a blessing. But often when the joys and gifts that we crave are granted to the person right in front of us, envy doesn't allow us to see straight. Envy is more than a desire to have what the other has; it is the sinister wish and angry hope that what they have might be taken away, or that they themselves might even be hurt. Our selfish, competitive yearnings make it so we can hardly bear the ways in which our rivals have been blessed. As an ancient church leader was quoted, "The envious person looks for but one remedy for his affliction: to see one of those he envies fall into misfortune."[25]

We've learned and can easily see that God is sovereign in choosing how He dispenses His diverse blessings to His creatures. Our innate appraisal of a giant hissing cockroach and a majestic Arabian horse can quickly prove this point. (And for you insect lovers, there is admittedly an important God-given role and a kind of glory reflected in every species of insect, but it is safe to say that virtually every fifteen-year-old daughter would rather have her parents give her a horse for her birthday than a terrarium full of cockroaches.) When it comes to human beings, our culture might be frantically attempting to protect everyone's feelings by trying to deny the varied glory of blessings that God bestows on people—but the reality is undeniable. We all innately understand, no matter how much we want to pretend, that God-given talents, intelligence, beauty, aptitude, strength, and skills, along with a long list of other gifts, clearly give advantages to one person over another.

The challenge comes when those superior endowments or achievements are enjoyed by the people I rub shoulders with all the time—my friends, my family members, the people that I say I love. Again, the ancient thinkers capture the experience of the problem: "I am envious and bitter: the gifts of my friends are a torment to me. I grieve at my brother's happiness."[26] Think of the logical contradictions in that description—friends/torment, brother/grieve. That irrational combination is an unmistakable sign that something is very wrong. And plainly there is. It's called envy! Thankfully there is a simple, though difficult, solution. It is so simple that I can state it in four words. But it is so challenging that I think one could write volumes in hopes of successfully driving it home in our lives. Ready? Here it comes!

## LOVE DOES NOT ENVY

First Corinthians 13:4 reads: "Love does not envy." Bam! There it is. The biblical solution in four words. Actually, I can say it in one—*love*! But though it is a common word that is thrown around everywhere, it is much easier said than done. Especially because what passes for love these days falls light-years short of what is being described in 1 Corinthians 13.

The context of this passage is likely a lot further from how we normally hear it quoted, and dead center in the middle of the topic we are discussing in this book. So, printed wedding reception napkins notwithstanding, I want you to think of the problems in first-century Corinth, and how God drops these words on them as the solution—and it wasn't at a wedding. Paul had sternly confronted their factionalism and tribalism. These Christians were acting like non-Christians. One Bible study group was saying, "We're of Paul!" and another was saying, "We're of Apollos!" and still others were saying, "We're of Peter!" while the super spiritual were saying, "Well, you losers, our group is of Christ!" (See 1 Cor. 1:10–13; 3:1–4.)

You can't have that kind of competitive spirit without plenty of jealousy, pride, selfishness, resentment, and envy. Paul says you guys are "puffed up in favor of one against another" (1 Cor. 4:6). They were taking each other to court (1 Cor. 6:6), there was vocalized belittlement of married couples by the singles, which Paul had to put to rest in chapter 7. These Christians were sinning against each other by pridefully flaunting their freedoms, and disparaging each other for where they shopped for groceries (1 Cor. 8:11–12). They had to be confronted for snubbing each other in their church services (chapter 11), and for all their subtle and overt rivalries over who had which roles and what offices, and who had the most important gifts (chapter 12).

Far from the romantic context of a tux-clad young man saying sweet things to his new bride, these verses were not penned for your pastor to read at your wedding; they were originally put on the table as the solution to a lot of junk enveloping the church and infecting the hearts of its professing Christians. These words about "love" were the antidote to what we have been trying to tackle in this book—the issues that stem from runaway envy.

## THE ANTITHESIS OF ENVY

This famous paragraph begins with a positive statement: "Love is patient and kind"—the things that were desperately lacking in the lives of these Christians. But it is the next phrase, the first negation on the list, that I contend is a summation of what would fix all the yuck that was contaminating these parishioners and dishonoring Christ. The next four words: "Love does not envy"! Think back to what we have learned about envy, and then let the cascade of the following negations flow: it does not "boast; it is not arrogant or rude. It does not insist on its own way; it is not irritable or resentful; it does not rejoice at wrongdoing" (1 Cor. 13:4b–6). It should not be hard to see that the eight things that love does not do all grow out of the first one—love does not envy.

It seems the leaders from church history that I have been quoting were onto something by making such a big deal of the sin of envy. They called it a deadly sin, or a capital sin, because it is such a primary problem, and a source from which so many other sins sprout. Once more, in the words of Cyprian of Carthage, "It is the root of all evils, the fountain of disasters, the nursery of crimes, the material of transgressions."[27] The problems pervading the Corinthian church, and so many of our churches today, can be traced back to this envious spirit. It is an irritable, resentful, arrogant disposition which boasts so that people know no one is outdoing me. It is rude because I'm resentful that you are advancing beyond me. It insists on its own way because, after all, why should you get to have me do it your way? And it confidentially rejoices when the ones I envy do wrong.

Here we have Christians treating the people they call their fellow members, friends, brothers, sisters, and neighbors as their rivals, competitors, and opponents. In 1 Corinthians 13, the Holy Spirit has inscribed as clearly as can be understood: you can't envy the ones you love. Or maybe I should turn that around for you. You don't love the ones you envy. So take a second to make that as personal as you can. Recall the faces that have already surfaced in your mind, those about whom you have already felt that pang of conviction. You know you envy them, because you have focused on this particular sin for a while now. See their faces? Mentally recite their names. Okay, here's the truth, Christian. You don't love them. You can call them your *friend*, your *sister*, your *team member*, and your *brother*, but that rings hollow in light of the Bible's diagnosis. You don't love them—but you can, and of course you should. The counterpunch to these envious feelings and annoyed attitudes is to love them. Which, I remind you, does not need to be preceded by warm feelings of affection. As a matter of fact, this is most needed when you don't have those warm feelings and affections. You need to *choose* to love them. Biblically. Resolutely. Any progress in loving them will automatically start to drive out envy. Why? Because love is antithetical to envy. They can't both exist at the same place and at the same time.

## CASE STUDY

A lot passes for love these days in our culture's music, movies, and on the dating scene, but in reality it has little correlation with what God is getting at in 1 Corinthians 13. Thankfully, by God's common grace and mercy, there is a gift of love that is widely distributed by Him to a large portion of the population. It can be a case study and serve as a corrective to our inclination for envy. The exemplary love that God dispenses is in part to guarantee the propagation of the human race; it is the love He pours out into the hearts of new parents.

Think about it. When a newborn is discharged from the hospital and fastidiously strapped into the infant car seat, those parents, who might have just days ago been self-absorbed and self-promoting individuals, suddenly find themselves snapping up out of bed at 2:00 a.m. to attend to Junior's every whimper, demand for a feeding, and screams for a diaper change. It doesn't matter how less-than-perfect or cantankerous their tot might be, they brag about their little cherub and applaud his every move. In most cases, the common grace of God suddenly infuses into these formerly lazy individuals something that moves them to become tireless servants, waiting on their baby hand and foot. They sacrifice, they spend money, they care, they praise, they bear all things, believe all things, hope all things, and endure all things.

As Junior begins to grow, and learn, and play sports, I'll tell you one thing the parents don't do—they don't envy their child. When Junior is named the student of the month, they don't begrudge him for it. They don't whisper behind his back and say, "I can't believe that kid got recognized for being a good student! I was a way better student that he was. If he thinks I'm going to his award ceremony, he's got another think coming." When their daughter is chosen to be the highlighted pianist at next Tuesday night's recital, the parents don't say, "I think I suddenly got busy next week. I'm not going to go and applaud for that girl; I think all this stuff is going to her head!" When their son scores the game-winning goal for his soccer team, the mom doesn't cross her arms, roll her eyes, turn to her best friend, and say, "Unbelievable! Look at all these people cheering for him! I'll bet he really thinks he's all that." When their son twists his ankle and is taken out of the game, Dad doesn't mutter, "Good, it's about time. He was just hotdogging out there, scoring all those goals."

That doesn't happen because "love does not envy." Love is not resentful, and it doesn't rejoice when misfortune overtakes a beloved child. It does just the opposite. Instead of wanting to make sure Junior doesn't outshine them, the people who love Junior always want Junior to outshine them. They want Junior to do better than they did. They want him to go further, to excel. And even if it is ten times more, they are all for it. It is not cause for envy, resentment, or sadness. It is cause for rejoicing and admiration. It is cause for satisfaction. Love seeks the good of the one who is loved. It hopes for the best in the life of the one who is loved. It seeks to aid the well-being and benefit of the one loved in any reasonable way possible.

Unfortunately, that is not how we think or feel about the brother in Christ who tells us he got three raises at work last year, when we only received one. It's not how we feel when we look at our best friends and they seem to get all the breaks that we don't get, all the compliments we don't hear, and achieve all the successes we only dream about. But those feelings could change if the intent of our minds and hearts moves from these people being just people in our lives to being people we have chosen to love.

## THE IMPORTANCE OF REAL LOVE

Mindset changes everything. And I do mean everything! A truly Christian mindset can transform even the Corinthian congregation into one that experiences the loving relationships that Paul lays out for the Philippian Christians. He describes it in Philippians 2:1 with four phrases: "So if there is any encouragement in Christ, any comfort from love, any participation in the Spirit, any affection and sympathy . . ."

When we tie the last two in the list together, and I believe we should, we have spelled out four experiences that are all derived from our vertical relationship with God. Look at it this way:

1. We are "encouraged"—heartened, shored up, made stronger by Christ and His presence in our lives, and the work accomplished for us in our redemption.
2. We are "comforted"—consoled, set right, granted peace by the fact that God loves us, and by what He has done to redeem us.
3. We have "participation"—acceptance, comradery, union in God's Spirit by His active presence in our lives because we are His.
4. We have "affection and sympathy"—we are internally moved, warmed, relieved, because of all the preceding realities related to God's merciful salvation.

The sentences that lead into this (Phil. 1:29–30) are some "we-are-all-in-this-together" verses about the struggles and conflicts we face as Christians in this world. So the emphasis of this list is the fact that these four gracious realities from God (i.e., encouragement, comfort, participation, and affection-sympathy) are all shared experiences that should band us together. While they are all vertical in that they come from God, they are all common experiences that we get to celebrate as a team down here on earth, and these truths should weld us together.

But there is one more important dimension to this list. It is highlighted by what comes next in verses 2–4. The horizontal dimension of these realities is found in the fact that God demonstrates the day-to-day experience of those vertical realities through our relationships with one another. In other words, the tangible expressions of Christ's "encouragement" come through my relationships with His people. I am to experience the "comfort" of God's love for me through rightly interacting with His children. The sense of "acceptance" and fellowship I have with our Redeemer is tangibly encountered through the welcome and mutual devotion of the body of Christ. And the feelings of "affection and sympathy" I enjoy, being the object of God's care, are brokered through the Christlike hands and feet of the band of redeemed and forgiven people that surround me.

Think about how Paul speaks of the agency of God's people being the conduit for him to enjoy a particular benefit that the Lord sought to accomplish for him. He says, "God, who comforts the downcast, comforted us by the coming of Titus" (2 Cor. 7:6). God is reaching out to "comfort" Paul (which is the same Greek word translated "encouragement" in Philippians 2:1), and yet the "comfort" or "encouragement" during this time of Paul being downcast is provided through the instrumentality of Titus—just a human being saved by grace and responsive to the way God wanted to use him. A few chapters earlier Paul had confessed to despairing even of life, but he resolved to be buoyed by the hope that he was an accepted child of God who could and would make it through his severe trial in Asia. He again demonstrates my point by what he states in the very next sentence: "You also must help us by prayer, so that many will give thanks on our behalf for the blessing granted us through the prayers of many" (2 Cor. 1:9–10).

I worked through the logic of Philippians 2:1 using just a couple of brief examples from 2 Corinthians to make the following point. Your role in loving those around you, especially the people of God who share the realities of your salvation, is critical. Your love, and whether or not it is actually present and functioning as it ought, is the means by which God generally allows His children to experience His love, acceptance, encouragement, and comfort. What thwarts that whole process? The resentment, competitiveness, or sorrowful withdrawal that comes from envy—these throw a major wrench in those gears. If you envy the people you are supposed to love, the very ones in whose lives God wants to use you to demonstrate His love, then the casualty is much greater than the quality of friendships you possess. You have become an obstacle to God's work in the lives of His children. That's not where you want to be. Vanquishing envy is more than the satisfaction of knowing that you truly love the people you think you love; it is a sanctified means of channeling God's love to others.

## LOVE'S MINDSET

Thankfully God uses the apostle Paul to teach us how this works and where our mindset needs to be if we are to love as we ought. It is a kind of love that makes us useful to God in the lives of others, and pummels our envy at the same time. Here is how it is described: "Do nothing from selfish ambition or conceit, but in humility count others more significant than yourselves. Let each of you look not only to his own interests, but also to the interests of others" (Phil. 2:3–4).

Those two sentences require a lot of mental recalibration. It is certainly not our default mindset. They are commands that leave the world scratching its head. It is a countercultural way to function—to put it mildly. But we must, as so much is riding on this. Our temptations to envy stand in stark contrast. There is no way to nurse an envious heart and carry out these instructions from God.

These two verses from Philippians are the grown-up version of what God illustrates so well in most parents of newborns. To care for their child, they must lay aside any selfish ambitions they might have on Saturday morning. And we must see that when it comes to our friends, coworkers, and in particular, our fellow Christians, we have to put our selfish ambitions in the back seat on any given Saturday morning, Tuesday night, or Thursday afternoon. As a new parent I can't utter what would be unthinkable, or even think for one minute, "I am more important than this little runt. My interests are obviously more important and must always come first!" No matter how "popular" and "successful" we understand the other people in our lives to be, we must sincerely ask, "How might I lovingly and sincerely be a blessing to her? How might I be the means through which God aids his life, advances his interests, and meets his needs?"

It is no surprise that this mindset includes a prohibition against conceit and a call to exercise humility. There is no way I can even begin to think this way unless I climb off my pedestal and stop looking down on the people I'm supposed to love. I must see their lives and their interests as worthy of my attention and effort.

Trust me, I know what you are thinking. *This seems like hyperbole. How can someone truly function like this? Wouldn't I become a doormat? Does God really want me to clean his garage? Am I expected to clean her toilets? Next, I'll be washing their feet. And I don't think I have any friends who love me back in a way even close to this. As a matter of fact, I think I have some people in my small group who would betray me if they had half a reason to!*

You saw what I did there. Did you picture Jesus with a basin of quickly browning water and a soaked towel, cradling Judas's dirty foot in His left hand as He kindly runs the wet towel between the grimy toes of His soon-to-be betrayer? Well, if you didn't, you do now. And Jesus said, "I have just given you an example" (John 13:15). The example was for us to follow. So, yes!—garages, toilets, hospital rooms, baby showers, their kids' piano recitals, and even their corporate promotion ceremonies. Going the extra mile, staying the extra hour, and spending the extra dollar do not make us doormats, unless we think being a servant makes us a doormat. And even if we do, let's be the best doormats we can be. Is it costly? Yes. Will we wonder at times, *Who will meet my needs, and who will care for me?* Yes. Does it eat away at our leisure time and reduce our hours on YouTube and Netflix? Yep. But it is the right mindset. Do you know why? Because the next verse in Philippians 2 tells us it was the mindset of Christ.

## THE ULTIMATE CASE STUDY

This won't take much elaboration. It is the central message of Christianity, and I trust you are familiar with it. So, let's just soak in the description of the mindset we are supposed to have, which was exemplified by Christ and leaves no room for the resentful, boastful, arrogant, competitive, self-focused fruit of envy:

Have this mind among yourselves, which is yours in Christ Jesus, who, though he was in the form of God, did not count equality with God a thing to be grasped, but emptied himself, by taking the form of a servant, being born in the likeness of men. And being found in human form, he humbled himself by becoming obedient to the point of death, even death on a cross. (Phil. 2:5–8)

The feeling that I am letting go of my own importance when I turn my back on envy and recalibrate my mind to be like Christ's is unavoidable. But it is also lauded as virtuous. It could not be more virtuous. Is it sacrificial? Of course. Does it risk me feeling empty? Yes. But this is the kicker: when we lay down our own self-importance and become servants who would gladly and with sincerity clean the toilets of the one we feel is advancing past us, then we are imitating the most God-pleasing life that ever walked the planet. We are reflecting the mind of Christ. It feels upside down, and counter to all the desires on display in our culture. But please remember, after describing the engrossing and pervasive desires and appetites of the world, 1 John 2:17 delivers the punchline: "The world is passing away along with its desires, but whoever does the will of God abides forever."

If you feel that any earnest and sustained adoption of this mindset will leave you being the chump of your church or friend group, keep Jesus' probing question and answer in view. And don't forget, He was the One who washed the feet of His friends—some who had illusions of grandeur, others who were namby-pamby, still others who were scheming behind His back. But here's what He asked: "For who is the greater, one who reclines at table or one who serves? Is it not the one who reclines at table? But I am among you as the one who serves" (Luke 22:27).

Seeing Jesus being the servant may look bad, humiliating, unfair, and just not right from our vantage point. But let's never forget how the challenge to truly love ends the Philippians 2 passage.

Therefore God has highly exalted him and bestowed on him the name that is above every name, so that at the name of Jesus every knee should bow, in heaven and on earth and under the earth, and every tongue confess that Jesus Christ is Lord, to the glory of God the Father. (Phil 2:9–11)

And while the parallels are not precise, when we choose the mindset of love over envy, they are not completely lost. God is always kind, generous, and proud of those who truly reflect His own love and servanthood. Allow me to end this chapter with the following heartening words, which I pray will get us past any rationalizations we may have, and move us to take the risk of truly loving the people in our lives:

For God is not unjust so as to overlook your work and the love that you have shown for his name in serving the saints, as you still do. And we desire each one of you to show the same earnestness to have the full assurance of hope until the end, so that you may not be sluggish, but imitators of those who through faith and patience inherit the promises. (Heb. 6:10–12)

# COUNTERATTACK ON ENVY: REJOICE

**After Jack Dempsey,** former heavyweight boxing champ, retired from the ring at the outset of World War II, he went on to serve his country in the Coast Guard. They wisely commissioned "Lieutenant Dempsey" to train troops for hand-to-hand combat. The step-by-step manual he created for commando fighting was published in 1942 and is still available online today. It sounds like they allowed the career boxer to word the title, which simply reads, *How to Fight Tough.*[28]

In this interesting photo-laden manual we hear Dempsey explain the oft-repeated line that "the best defense is a good offense."[29] We also pick up some of his other unvarnished tips, which churn in the mind of someone who beats people up for a living. Lines like, "Softness is suicide," "Kill or be killed," "He who strikes last dies first."[30] These are not bad reminders for Christians who have been warned by God that the Christian life is a battle. And that we have a ferocious enemy, along with a myriad of evil henchmen, who would like to obstruct God's work in and through our lives, and even destroy us completely if they were allowed. But unlike Dempsey's manual, our counterattacks don't look like the world's. "For the weapons of our warfare," the Bible says, "are not of the flesh" (2 Cor. 10:4). That's why the titles of this chapter and the last seem so oxymoronic and paradoxical. How does one beat back vicious spiritual attackers and their tactics with love and rejoicing? Well, we do. Effectively. Love and rejoicing may not be conventional weaponry found in the history of warfare. But that does not mean they do not have, as 2 Corinthians 10:4 goes on to say, "divine power to destroy strongholds." They do divinely break apart the selfish, competitive, satanic ways of thinking that our spiritual enemies so badly want us to settle into. We should, as the Commander's children, tap into "the power of God; with the weapons of righteousness for the right hand and for the left" (2 Cor. 6:7). So let us consider the envy-defeating righteous weapon of rejoicing.

## REJOICE WITH THOSE WHO REJOICE

You are good at rejoicing in the wake of your own job promotion, your own new car, your own child's achievements, your own good health, and your own Christmas bonus—you get the point. Something that gives you advantages, blesses you, rewards you, or awards you innately makes you happy. And that is a thoroughly Christian expectation, despite the familiar yet misleading Christian adage that you are supposed to "aim for joy, not happiness."[31] Being happy is good. But as Jesus might well have put it, "If you are only happy for your own blessings, what reward do you have? Do not even the tax collectors do the same?" The challenge is for you to rejoice with others who have cause for rejoicing. And there's the rub; it is most certainly a different story when the blessing that is causing my friend to rejoice is a blessing I don't have.

While writing that last paragraph I was interrupted by a text from my friend, who wrote that he had a lead on a new house. He, like so many apartment-dwellers in high-rent coastal California, has been priced out of the market for years. Well, my friend got a decent raise, and was just walking with the realtor through a "real" house: one with four independent walls not attached to any neighbors, a spacious two-car garage, and an actual driveway (that's a grade-A blessing for these parts). He put in an offer, asked for prayer, and said he thinks he and his family are going to get it. I couldn't help but gush for him. I literally texted him ten lines of rephrased and heartfelt congratulations. But here's the thing—God has already been gracious to me by allowing me to live in a real house. It took me thirteen years of living here before I could land one, but I actually did. And in clicking through the pictures of my friend's prospective house, I think our kitchen is bigger. So, how hard was it really for me to go on and on about how sincerely happy I am for them? Not too hard. I love them, but it really wasn't the kind of good news and prayer request for closing the deal that would tempt me to not "rejoice with my buddy who is rejoicing."

On the other hand, I know several (even a few of our mutual friends who live in adjacent apartment complexes) who would read the first line of his text and immediately be tempted to not share the joy I just demonstrated. And I know if I could go back in time and watch my younger self read that text, maybe somewhere in the eighth year of my challenging season of trying to scrimp and save in a seemingly impossible Southern California housing market, I'm pretty sure Satan's emissaries would be poised to pounce on me with a truckload of temptation to envy. It certainly would not be reflexive to gush with fraternal joy over his good news. I'd have to dig deep in my heart and find the place where true Christian love for my friends resides. And frightfully, if it were the eleventh year of that cramped season of my life and growing family's experience, I wonder if I could have passed the test at all.

## HARD TO BE HAPPY?

The command to be happy in Romans 12:15 is exceedingly hard in those kinds of situations. To share another personal challenge from our past, my wife and I were ten years into our marriage before we had our first child. We struggled with infertility for years, and my wife submitted herself to two surgeries in hopes of making the desire of holding our babies in her arms possible. During these protracted treatments and monthly disappointments, which seemed to drag on forever, you can imagine how many of our close friends in the same age range were popping out babies left and right. How many baby showers did my wife go shopping for, dress for, drive to, and participate in? I couldn't tell you, but she and I felt every single one of them. It was a hard command to truly and sincerely love our friends and acquaintances enough to genuinely rejoice when they were rejoicing. The success or failure of our love for our circle of friends was often measured by how many baby showers she was invited to. All it took was a little insincerity to throw the spotlight on our deprivation. People who didn't want to hurt our feelings—often because our feelings seeped through our perfunctory "congrats"—just thought it better not to send us their birth announcements or invite us to their one-year-old's birthday party. The task for us, and many of you, is a kind of real selfless love that is intentional and demonstrative about rejoicing and celebrating other people's wins. So much so that no one in your friend circle would feel it was really a celebration unless the expert "rejoicer" was at the party.

Many read all of Romans 12:15, which says, "Rejoice with those who rejoice, weep with those who weep" and simplistically think it would be harder to join in with the sorrow of those in pain than it would be to join in the rejoicing of those who are celebrating, just because one is a negative emotion and the other a positive one. But that is not true. Not even close. Think a minute about being in the middle of this chapter and getting a call from a friend you work with in your office, or a mom of one of the kids on your son's little league team. If they told you there had been a terrible accident and that their family members were all on life support at the hospital down the road, how hard would it be for you to get your jacket on, run to their side, and weep with them as they clutch the hands of their dying loved ones? Answer: not hard. Only the most callous among us would see that as a drudgery, a burden, or something they'd have to dig deep to accomplish. But if you turn this around to rejoicing with those who rejoice, based on the example we have been considering, it is far more difficult. Yet, it is what God expects from His people, who are loved by Him and called to channel that divine love through their relationships.

Who wouldn't expect hard and counterintuitive commands in Romans 12? Have you read this section of Scripture lately? Listen to the preceding verse: "Bless those who persecute you; bless and do not curse them" (v. 14). You can pick up a clue as to the difficulty of this directive by its repetition. Similar to when, on Saturday morning, my dad would say, "I know you have a game today, but you have to cut the grass—I know you want to ride off to the field, but you've got to do it; you have to cut it." He would say something like that when he knew I didn't want to do it. It was when he knew everything in me wanted to open the garage door and walk to my bike and *not* the lawnmower. The repetition, raised eyebrows, and slow nod, all made the point—"You may not feel like doing it, but this is nonnegotiable." In Romans 12:14 you can hear God saying, "I know you don't want to bless them, and I realize everything in you wants to lash out and curse them back, but you have to bless them, not curse them—you've got to do it."

Romans 12:17 continues with more counterintuitive instructions, "Repay no one evil for evil." Then verse 19, "Never avenge yourselves." And verse 20, "To the contrary, 'if your enemy is hungry, feed him; if he is thirsty, give him something to drink." It doesn't get much harder than that. Except maybe running off to your third bridal shower party in six weeks, after your boyfriend called off your engagement and dumped you. Ouch! Picking out a gift for the bride-to-be, penning words of joyful congratulations, and playing the bachelorette games with a happy smile on your face feels, I would guess, about the same. We all have our own versions of that scenario. They should remind us that this call to rejoice is undoubtedly one of the hardest types of situations in which we Christians are commanded to be happy, to rejoice, and to celebrate. But when we do, we are leaving no room for the deadly sin of envy to germinate in our hearts.

## EVERY GOOD GIFT

One perspective that I trust will help to direct and fuel obedience to this difficult command is a little verse found in James 1:17a. It simply reads, "Every good gift and every perfect gift is from above, coming down from the Father." Let the implications of that sink in. Here we are reminded that everything that is good, every "perfect gift" as it is called, comes from God. "Perfect" here, by the way, is a translation of the Greek word *teleios*, which is used in a variety of contexts in the New Testament to connote the sense that some gift is "just right," it "hits the spot," it is "just as you would want it to be."

Back to my house for just a minute. Like most people with houses in this part of the country, the purchase of my house has a story. I won't tell it all, but clearly God was maneuvering and positioning this house to be the house that would be *just right* for our family. We were raising three kids and desired a few things that would be ideal to check all the boxes for our two rambunctious boys, our disabled daughter, and our busy ministry schedule. This house was it. As I have said to God in thanksgiving so many times, "Thank You God, this house is perfect for us!" That's the sense of *teleios*. If you were to listen to my preaching, you would quickly learn that I don't mean "perfect" as in "without defect." The imperfections of my house have provided my exposition with plenty of illustrative material. I couldn't even get through this book without telling you about the trees that line our driveway and their surreptitious roots that have chipped away at our savings account.

With that said, I am sure you know of a lot of things your friends and fellow Christians have acquired that are just right for them. These particular blessings check all the boxes for some area of their lives. The gifts are the kind that hit the spot and bring the "ahhhhh" sense of satisfaction to their hearts, so that there would be no temptation to look for a replacement. For some it's their home, for others it's their job, or their spouse, their income, their church, etc. These are the things that provoke the envy of others, whose bitterness amplifies as they think, *Look at that! All the doors in her life fling open. He's got everything. She gets all the breaks.*

Back to James 1:17. The point I'm trying to highlight here is that these blessings are emphatically stated to be given to them by God. The Lord granted them. It was the Sovereign King you prayed to this morning who lavished those blessings on them. It was the Redeemer to whom you heartily sang last Sunday morning who reached out and placed that good gift in their life. We often read James 1:17 with our own lives in view, and it helps us sing with heartfelt sincerity about how gracious God has been to us personally. But this is also true for the woman or man sitting across the aisle whose life you envy, along with all the distinctions between you and them that enflame your resentful bitterness. The gifts in their lives that bring you sadness or torment have all been granted to them by your God. The first half of 1 Corinthians 4:7 states it succinctly, "For who sees anything different in you? What do you have that you did not receive?" Whether you are the "have" or the "have not" in that verse, the gifts come from your Father.

Let me state it this way. The difference between you and the one you envy is your Father in heaven. The "beef" you feel so justified in nursing is really with the wrong person. Which I hope, in stating, gives you pause. When you get hostile or harsh toward the one who has what you want, you need to remember they wouldn't have it if God hadn't granted it to them. See that clearly, and then ask yourself, "Is this really a beef I want to take up with God?"

It was God who had graciously gifted Leah a healthy child, for which Rachel "envied" her (Gen. 30:1a). Rachel envied her so much she screamed out to Jacob her husband, "Give me children, or I shall die!" (v. 1b). Even though the following retort was hurled at Rachel in frustration and anger by Jacob, he actually hit the nail on the head: "Am I in the place of God, who has withheld from you the fruit of the womb?" (v. 2b). Probably not the most loving delivery as the first half of that verse makes clear, but you can't argue with the sentiment. This was a God thing, not a Jacob thing, and certainly not a Leah thing. Rachel's hatred toward Leah and her baby boy as well as her frustration at her husband were the ugly fruits of an envious heart that needed to understand that this is dealt with in prayer, and resolved in a dialogue with God, not in hostilities, gossip, or acrimony toward anyone else.

The gargantuan challenge for Rachel, and for us, is to marshal our thoughts, words, and actions to do what God says is right, and best, and profitable. And at this point we know what that is. We need to evaluate our feelings, sort them out, choose to love the ones we are tempted to envy, and consciously celebrate the gifts that God—who we say we love—has chosen to grant to them and not us. That is a big challenge for sure. Especially when everything else within us screams, *Just do what you feel.* Which in this case results in more covetousness, more bitterness, more jealousy, and more dissension.

## BUT I DON'T FEEL IT!

I understand why we struggle to do the things we don't feel like doing. It happens to me early every morning when the alarm goes off. But we must concede that so much of our lives are filled with things that must be done—regardless of whether we feel like it or not. Our self-destructive culture and its call to enthrone our feelings and passions in the captain's seat of our lives is folly to the highest degree. We really don't want to see our world, our country, our churches, our families, or our own lives characterized by doing whatever it is we feel. Not only civil order but biblical righteousness depends on turning a deaf ear to our screaming emotions. This is fundamental to doing what is right. It is why Jesus was clear that following Him, His path, His teaching, and the dictates of what is pleasing to the Father, and in the end good for us, is going to require plenty of self-denial. "If anyone would come after me," Jesus said, "let him deny himself" (Luke 9:23). The baseline expectation is that to be a Christian is to accept an invitation to an internal battle. "Abstain from the passions of the flesh, which wage war against your soul," 1 Peter 2:11 tells us. These eruptions of envious conflicts and bitterness in our relationships don't happen without us letting up on the fight inside our own hearts. Remember the question and answer of James 4:1? "What causes quarrels and what causes fights among you? Is it not this, that your passions are at war within you?" The disorder and transgression that characterize our world are diagnosed with these words: "They have become callous and have given themselves up to sensuality, greedy to practice every kind of impurity" (Eph. 4:19).

We obviously can't go with the flow of our impulses and preferences. As Christians, we have been enabled by God's Spirit to have a real break with the old patterns. As imperfectly as we proceed, the next verse in Ephesians 4 tells us, "But that is not the way you learned Christ!" (v. 20). The passage goes on to remind us that "the truth is in Jesus" and it calls us "to put off your old self, which belongs to your former manner of life and is corrupt through deceitful desires, and to be renewed in the spirit of your minds, and to put on the new self, created after the likeness of God in true righteousness and holiness" (vv. 21b–24). That is a deliberate and continual act. It wouldn't matter if this book were about the vice of drugs, alcohol, porn, or kleptomania, the practice is the same. We have to engage in a volitional resolve to live in keeping with Christ's values and turn our backs on the particular vice that has its hooks in us. And then march forward to live in tight step with Christ. As our passage states, it is to "put on the new self," the new life that God has granted to real Christians, which is "created in the likeness of God" and always craves, at a core level, "true righteousness and holiness." We just have to bust through the din of emotions that are yelling at us to do the contrary.

## PRACTICE MAKES PROBLEMS FOR ENVY

In one of my favorite passages, David has a talk with himself. He inscribed the conversation in the lyrics of a song.

> Bless the LORD, O my soul,
>     and all that is within me,
>     bless his holy name!
> Bless the LORD, O my soul,
>     and forget not all his benefits,
> who forgives all your iniquity,
>     who heals all your diseases,
> who redeems your life from the pit,
>     who crowns you with steadfast love and mercy,
> who satisfies you with good
>     so that your youth is renewed like the eagle's.
> (Ps. 103.1–5)

This is so helpful. David shows us a direct and pretty pushy relationship with himself. He does not coddle his feelings nor let his soul do whatever it feels like doing. He is going to tell his soul what to do. In this case, he is going to tell his soul to bow before his God and be thankful. He tells his soul to take stock of all that God has done for him. He tells his own soul to take an inventory. Not for the sake of comparison, but for the sake of thanksgiving. Every good and just-right gift comes from the Lord, so he tells himself he has lots for which to be thankful. He says there's sicknesses in his rearview mirror. He says he's been delivered out of many past troubles. He has gifts from the Lord that have been satisfying. There have been plenty of days and plenty of things for which he can be profoundly and sincerely thankful.

It's a heart like this that can begin to honestly say, "I have one gift, and you have a different one; that's great, God is good" (cf. 1 Cor. 7:7). Different gifts, but the same God who is Lord of them all (1 Cor. 12:6). This practice not only sets us up to "chill out" about what we *don't* have, but it also helps us do what we are told to do about the gifts of others. Rejoice! "Hey soul, they just had a baby, *rejoice*! Hey soul, they just got a house, *rejoice*! Hey soul, God has given that woman so many great things, *rejoice*! Hey soul, that guy did an amazing job on his sales numbers this quarter, *rejoice*! Hey soul, that kid does so well and brings so much joy to his parents, *rejoice*! Hey soul, that man was given an amazing dream job, *rejoice*!"

We have to get in the habit of regularly pulling out all the stops and celebrating the blessings and accomplishments of those around us—without any self-pity or hints of comparisons. This is not like the deceitful and "profuse . . . kisses of an enemy" (Prov. 27:6). This is not flattery or a quest to be seen by others as magnanimous. When you see any of that starting to creep up, it's time to lecture your soul. As true Christians, we have the capacity to adopt Christ's mindset. It is ours in Christ Jesus. We have a new heart that has been made in the image of its Creator, and because of Christ we can fight and put to death the warring passions of envy (Col. 3:5). We can do this. We must do this. It really isn't optional. It is commanded. Even the specific discipline to praise, honor, celebrate, affirm, and rejoice over the endowments of God in others' lives—not separating them from their gifts because it's supposedly your job to make sure they don't get a big head.

"A woman who fears the LORD is to be praised"—by you, even if there is already a crowd praising her for the distinctive godliness and grace that God has granted her (Prov. 31:28, 30b).

Respect should be expressed to those in high offices in the church and they should be esteemed "very highly in love because of their work"—by you, even if they have already heard multiple times this week how their God-given gifts have been a blessing to others (1 Thess. 5:12–13).

Recognition should be given to those who have been granted the courage by God to do things for the gospel and the good of others—by you, even if you would lack the valor to even try such things but secretly wish you could (Rom. 16:3–4).

Respect should go to whom respect is due, and honor should go to whom honor is due—even if it was the pagan king Nebuchadnezzar—knowing full well that every last ounce of his authority was undeservingly granted to him by God (Rom. 13:7; Dan. 2:37–38).

Time to rejoice. There are plenty of opportunities afforded by the lives of those around you. After you take stock of your own blessings and praise God for His kindness to you—for the sake of your own spiritual health, throw the spotlight on others. God's grace is varied. He dishes out His blessing in various ways and in varying degrees. Find someone today who has much for which to be thankful, and get to work in rejoicing with those who rejoice!

# EPILOGUE:
# A LOOK AHEAD

**A few years ago,** I wrote a book about heaven, hell, and the afterlife.[32] In it, I thought it necessary to very briefly address the absence of the particular sin we have been studying in this book. If you think about it, of course there will be no sin in the Christian's eternal home, but I had to single out coveting, jealousy, and envy in a small section of that book because of our near inability to even remotely imagine ourselves as people who wouldn't envy. When I presented the biblical material on the varying rewards in heaven, and the various levels of glory and acclaim given to some and not to others, I realized there was no way people could ponder this without a visceral objection that these things would make the New Jerusalem a terrible place to live.

I anticipated the objections from the readers because I have received them many times in person when I preached on these biblical promises. I heard, "How can some people have extensive rewards, high reputations, expansive authority, and big plots of real estate granted to them by God, and others get less? That wouldn't be fair!" But what they really mean by those objections is, "I'd be consumed with envy if I know that there are people in heaven who get to enjoy more blessings than I do!" But we must remember:

In the eternal state, we will all reside in glorified bodies. Our plotting spiritual enemy will be consigned to punishment, never to bother us again. We will sincerely and in every situation rejoice with those who have greater blessings than us.[33]

In short, you won't envy!

### Foretastes of Home

It was my prayer that on the preceding pages you would be able to envision what it would be like in your current life to push back against the destructive sin of envy in various situations, relationships, and settings. I certainly wanted to give you a clear mental picture of what the experience might be if you were able to sincerely rejoice with those whom you had previously envied; that you could see what true Christian love might look like toward those you currently resent; and that you could envision a heart, a family, a church, and a subculture that successfully fought envy and took back the ground lost to this sin.

If you saw some of that in your mind's eye, I want to have you biblically daydream about the place we are going. Our eternal home is like that—times a thousand. No sin. No temptation. No failure. No transgression. No hearts stirred to envy. I want you to consider all that comes with this:

"He will wipe away every tear from their eyes, and death shall be no more, neither shall there be mourning, nor crying, nor pain anymore, for the former things have passed away." And he who was seated on the throne said, "Behold,

I am making all things new." Also he said, "Write this down, for these words are trustworthy and true." (Rev. 21:4–5)

I want the image of a place where all of the world's sin is behind you to motivate you to fight the good fight. I want that envisioned, promised reality to recur in your life as an impetus to double down on experiencing some of that now—this week, this month, and this year. I want the hope and thought of that future joy to drive you to want to experience more foretastes of the absence of envy now. Hear afresh the words of 1 John 3:2–3:

Beloved, we are God's children now, and what we will be has not yet appeared; but we know that when he appears we shall be like him, because we shall see him as he is. And everyone who thus hopes in him purifies himself as he is pure.

## PEACETIME IS COMING

Those present moments of victory, which I hope will increase after you finish reading this book, are all going to be hard fought, something I sought to emphasize. Maybe so much so that you grew weary of the battle, boxing, and fighting motifs. Well, that was intentional. I want you to long for the time when you will hear the fulfilled call to "Beat your plowshares into swords, and your pruning hooks into spears; let the weak say, 'I am a warrior'" (Joel 3:10). That day is coming. When not only the external battles will be over but the internal battles will be over as well.

All our feelings of weakness in the throes of temptation's battles, and all the mental vigilance we need in this spiritual war against our enemy and his demonic snipers that are seeking to trip us up, will one day be behind us. Peace is coming and will be inaugurated by the Prince of Peace. He will win by vanquishing our foes and transforming our flesh with all of its ugly impulses. So fight on—for now. One day we will echo Paul's parting words,

I have fought the good fight, I have finished the race, I have kept the faith. Henceforth there is laid up for me the crown of righteousness, which the Lord, the righteous judge, will award to me on that day, and not only to me but also to all who have loved his appearing. (2 Tim. 4:7–8)

## DON'T DESPAIR, KEEP GOING

Keep plowing. Thank God for every single gain. And don't ever get despondent over the setbacks. "The righteous falls seven times and rises again" (Prov. 24:16a). Don't stay down. Get some accountability in your life to share the burden of the battle and keep striving to defeat this ugly sin. Don't give up—ever. Run through the tape and finish your course. No matter how hard the warfare rages, and no matter how often you feel like you've confessed the same sin over and over. Don't stop praying, trusting, wrestling, and confessing. "Work out your own salvation with fear and trembling, for it is God who works in you, both to will and to work for his good pleasure" (Phil. 2:12–13). God wants to see progress in this area of your life. So keep at it. Don't lean back. Don't take your foot off the gas pedal. You are going to make it and God will get you through, and may it be with less and less envy, and much more genuine love.

And it is my prayer that your love may abound more and more, with knowledge and all discernment, so that you may approve what is excellent, and so be pure and blameless for the day of Christ, filled with the fruit of righteousness that comes through Jesus Christ, to the glory and praise of God. (Phil. 1:9–11)

# NOTES

1. Mette Ivie Harrison, "Declaring War on Christian Metaphors," Huffpost.com, October 11, 2016, https://www.huffpost.com/entry/declaring-war-on-christiain_b_12428856.

2. Thomas Aquinas, *Summa Theologica: Complete English Edition in Five Volumes*, vol. 3, trans. Fathers of the English Dominican Province (New York: Benzinger Brothers, 1948), 1342–46.

3. Flavius Josephus, *The Works of Josephus: Complete and Unabridged*, updated ed., trans. William Whiston (Peabody, MA: Hendrickson, 1987), 608.

4. C. S. Wolcott, "Pilate Cycle," in *The Lexham Bible Dictionary*, ed. John D. Barry (Bellingham, WA: Lexham Press, 2016).

5. Fredrick W. Danker et al., *A Greek-English Lexicon of the New Testament and Other Early Christian Literature*, 3rd ed. (Chicago: University of Chicago Press, 2000), 199.

6. St. Augustine, *The Problem of Free Choice*, trans. Dom Mark Pontifex (Westminster, MD: Newman Press, 1955), 219.

7. William Law, *The Works of the Reverend William Law*, vol. 4 (London: J. Richardson, 1762), 183.

8. John Chrysostom, *Saint Chrysostom: Homilies on the Acts of the Apostles and the Epistle to the Romans*, A Select Library of the

Nicene and Post-Nicene Fathers, vol. 11, ed. Philip P. Schaff (New York: The Christian Leadership Co., 1889), 381.

9. Cyprian of Carthage, "On Jealousy and Envy," in *Hippolytus, Cyprian, Caius, Novatian*, The Ante-Nicene Fathers, vol. 5, eds. Alexander Roberts and James Donaldson (New York: Christian Literature Co., 1886), 492.

10. Rick Brannan et al., *The Lexham English Septuagint* (Bellingham, WA: Lexham Press, 2012), 847. *The Book of Wisdom*, its Latin title, is also known as the *Wisdom of Solomon*, which is a part of the non-canonical collection of books commonly referred to as the Old Testament Apocrypha. *The Book of Wisdom* is presented as a later expression of the insights of King Solomon and is generally dated to the first century before Christ.

11. R. Albert Mohler Jr., *Words from the Fire: Hearing the Voice of God in the 10 Commandments* (Chicago: Moody Publishers, 2009), 184–85.

12. Tilly Dillehay, *Seeing Green: Don't Let Envy Color Your Joy* (Eugene, OR: Harvest House, 2018), 40.

13. Groucho Marx, *Groucho and Me* (London: Muriwai Books, 2017), 143–44.

14. Joseph Epstein, *Envy: The Seven Deadly Sins* (New York: Oxford University Press, 2003), 1.

15. For instance, 1 Clement 45:7, which is enlisted as a description of the cruel and idolatrous men who threw Shadrach, Meshach, and Abednego into the fiery furnace.

16. See my chapter against the Roman Catholic doctrine of purgatory: "On My Way to Heaven I'll Have to Put in Some Time in Purgatory," in *10 Mistakes People Make about Heaven, Hell, and the Afterlife* (Eugene, OR: Harvest House Publishers, 2018), 51–59.

17. Tunku Varadarajan, "Jonathan Haidt on the 'National Crisis' of Gen Z," *Wall Street Journal*, December 30, 2022, https://www.wsj.com/articles/the-national-crisis-of-generation-z-jonathan-haidt-social-media-performance-anxiety-fragility-gap-childhood-11672401345.

18. *The Ed Sullivan Show*, January 11, 1970, https://youtu.be/p88LY_IQBh0.

19. Robert G. Robins, "Reasons of State—The Thirty Years' War, Europe's Last Religious War," *Christian History* 122 (2017): 28, https://christianhistoryinstitute.org/magazine/article/reasons-of-state.

20. "Lessons from Charlie Munger at the 2022 DJCO Meeting," Novel investor.com, February 18, 2022, https://novelinvestor.com/lessons-from-charlie-munger-at-the-2022-djco-meeting/; and video, https://youtu.be/20M26u0kFzE.

21. See my discussion about the "stars-in-my-eyes kids" and the "you-can-do-anything parents" in my book *Raising Men, Not Boys: Shepherding Your Sons to Be Men of God* (Chicago: Moody Publishers, 2017).

22. William Law, *A Serious Call to a Devout and Holy Life* (London: Charles Ewer, 1818), 240.

23. See my book *Lifelines for Tough Times: God's Presence and Help When You Hurt* (Eugene, OR: Harvest House, 2014).

24. Jack Dempsey, *How to Fight Tough: 100 Action Photos Teaching U.S. Commando Fighting* (Budoworks, 2022), 56.

25. St. Basil, as quoted by Dennis Okholm, *Dangerous Passions, Deadly Sins: Learning from the Psychology of Ancient Monks* (Grand Rapids: Brazos Press, 2014), 124.

26. St. Basil, as quoted by Christine D. Pohl, *Living into Community: Cultivating Practices That Sustain Us* (Grand Rapids, MI: Eerdmans, 2012), 45.

27. Cyprian of Carthage, "On Jealousy and Envy," 492.

28. Jack Dempsey, *How to Fight Tough*, 11.

29. Ibid., 56.

30. Ibid., Preface, 1.

31. Randy Alcorn, *Happiness* (Carol Stream, IL: Tyndale House Publishers, 2015), 35–40. Note the author's very helpful corrective to this misperception, especially as he enlists the support of so many Christian leaders throughout church history, including Edwards, Whitefield, Augustine, Pascal, Ryle, Broadus, and many more.

32. Mike Fabarez, *10 Mistakes People Make About Heaven, Hell, and the Afterlife* (Eugene, OR: Harvest House, 2018).

33. Ibid., 98.

## COMPASS
### BIBLE CHURCH

Compass Bible Church was planted in Orange County, California, in 2005, and is committed to reaching people for Christ, teaching people to be like Christ, and training people to serve Christ.

LEARN MORE AT WWW.COMPASSCHURCH.ORG

**COMPASS**
**BIBLE INSTITUTE**

**FOCAL POINT**
MINISTRIES

Compass Bible Institute, founded by Pastor Mike Fabarez and Compass Bible Church in Aliso Viejo, provides thorough biblical education and hands-on training to prepare individuals for leadership in Christian ministry. CBI offers full degrees, certificates, and graduate level courses with credits transferring to partnering colleges, universities, and seminaries.

COMPASSBIBLEINSTITUTE.ORG

Focal Point Radio Ministries is the Bible teaching ministry of Dr. Mike Fabarez. Since 1998 Focal Point has been proclaiming the depths of Scripture on the radio, online, and in print. Focal Point can be heard on over 800 outlets across the United States. Access to the radio program, sermons and devotionals is also available through the Focal Point App.

FOCALPOINTMINISTRIES.ORG

CCPA

COMPASS CHURCH PLANTING ASSOCIATION

NATIONAL EQUIPPED CONFERENCE

The Compass Church Planting Association is an association of churches committed to working hard at replicating more churches that highlight and promote the expository preaching of God's word.

COMPASSCHURCHPLANTING.ORG

The National Equipped Conference is designed to provide Christians with biblical instruction and practical motivation to effectively live the Christian life and fruitfully serve God's Church. The NEC is a biennial event, hosted by the Compass Church Planting Association.

EQUIPPEDCONFERENCE.COM